Catholic Light

Beauty Through the Seasons for the Spiritual Retreat

By

Anthony Bialobryski

PublishAmerica
Baltimore

© 2005 by Anthony Bialobryski.
All rights reserved. No part of this book may be reproduced, stored in a retrieval system or transmitted in any form or by any means without the prior written permission of the publishers, except by a reviewer who may quote brief passages in a review to be printed in a newspaper, magazine or journal.

First printing

At the specific preference of the author, PublishAmerica allowed this work to remain exactly as the author intended, verbatim, without editorial input.

ISBN: 1-4137-8286-8
PUBLISHED BY PUBLISHAMERICA, LLLP
www.publishamerica.com
Baltimore

Printed in the United States of America

For Sister Joanie Eppinga

I also acknowledge the aid of the following people:

Father Robert Egan
Don O'Connor
Mary O'Connor
Peter Cain
Dan Varnell
Bro. Joshua Seidl
Enya Brennan

Table of Contents

Preface

This is a book for those in the Church desiring holy refreshment. Its format is simple and short, since people who make a retreat should be seeking to jettison care, and so, should not be expecting to tackle a complex assignment. Yet, while it is suited to formal retreat, this book may be useful at home, in moments of private reflection. The very nature of this book, in fact, invites reflection.

I desire that the reader find my work to be, at very least, pleasant and intriguing; but ideally, I hope it will convey a palpable refreshment. Towards this latter end, I recommend that it be read in one extended session, if possible, as friends report advantages to this. And as with any kind of reading task, this is likely best achieved in solitude. But the benefit of this (or of any spiritual endeavor labeled "Christian") does not necessitate one's permanent withdrawal--nor should it.

Illustration of this truth is found among religious in the Church, who periodically withdraw--even from their own community--later to rejoin their friends, to share their individual experience and to offer spiritual direction to the laity. Religious life, professional or lay, is meant to be an enterprise of service, and the purpose of one's personal withdrawal is designed to be the *sharing* of its fruits with those around us. In my opinion, re-acknowledgment of this approach is fitting for today, for one important reason. Emphasis on keeping and developing our sense of church community has been advanced, in many ways (although probably not consciously), by offering the option of community against the option of an inner life with God.

This is natural, since interiority is often linked with isolation, and hence, with personal absorption. However, it is possible to cultivate interiority--anything from loneliness, anxiety, or even clinical depression, to prayerful fellowship with God--while in the presence of our friends. This truth has been confirmed for centuries by Catholic religious, and by spiritual directors in our time, some of whom describe their interaction with directees as compatible with (and even *simultaneous to*) an attitude of prayer, an attitude I hope this volume will facilitate.

In retreat this book will be intoxicating. A densely atmospheric mood, created through the use of rich liturgical and literary imagery, flows throughout the text, infusing its progression with a sense of color, of timelessness, and of holy mystery. It is also thought provoking, addressing many of the issues that the Christian ponders in retreat. To some, this volume may resemble something of a modern *Book of Hours*--a *Book of Catholic Seasons*, illuminated solely with the written word. The text, in fact, is geared to simulate the passage of the Christian year, and of the Christian life, done well. May it be a blessing to you all!

A.B.

Introduction

Often rarefied in substance and in tone, the language of aesthetics can express a longing and an awe for the ethereal, in the experience of nature, of personal reflection, and in our close relationships. It may also help convey the awesome presence of our God. But works of art deemed non-religious by an artist, are oft ascribed a spiritual significance by others. As a consequence of this, some discussions of aesthetics focus on addressing these dimensions.

Like everyone, I have my personal (and I stress personal) criterion for communicating and discerning God's charisma through the language of aesthetics. Amidst the sometimes dizzying plurality of views in Catholic dialogue, this threshold seems both grounded *and* exciting. It is concordant with the scripture texts of John, and based upon a venerated concept of the Church--and, it is delightfully transcendent. It is manifested, for this writer, in experience of light and revelation, occurring simultaneously, in the appreciation of, among other things, nature, of formal art, or in the liturgy.

This perspective formed the basis of the Gothic stained glass church. These luminous cathedrals were, in fact, envisioned to be analogues for New Jerusalem, and as such, were constructed on the theme of elemental purity. In his book *Passing Strange and Wonderful*, Yi-Fu Tuan writes: "The root inspiration of the cathedral was the Celestial Jerusalem of the book of Revelation... the Celestial City was a jewel of jewels, wrapped in light and color."[1] But, believes Tuan, this inspiration was not static, but rather, had a manifold effect on Christian populations of medieval Europe.

He illustrates the consequence of everyday exposure to this imagery (which contradicted, utterly, the harsh reality outside the church environment) as being overwhelming, and yet, that was buffered by a sense of sweet assurance: "When medieval people of strong faith entered a cathedral at the moment sunlight burst through the clouds and struck the rose window, making it glow, their feelings of joy and holy calm could be encompassed by language, if at all, only if it was mystical-religious rather than narrowly aesthetic. Medieval believers expected to find, upon dying and entering heaven, a reality with which they were already familiar." [2]

The driving force behind the renovation of the abbey church of St. Denis (the first authentic stained-glass Gothic church), Abbot Suger, was a man who recognized the spiritual potential of aesthetics in the church. In his writing he discloses: "I see myself dwelling, as it were, in some strange region of the universe which exists neither entirely in the slime of the earth nor entirely in the purity of Heaven; and... by the grace of God, I can be transported from this inferior to that higher world." [3]

In seeking more contemporary (and accessible) examples of this grand experience, and to sample a degree of its effect, one need only read a passage from *The Heritage of the Cathedral* by Sartell Prentice:

> The sun, streaming through the windows of Chartres Cathedral, of Bourges, or of Poiters, receives, as it comes, the color of the ruby, the amethyst, the sapphire, or the emerald in colors so rich that men have called the windows "jeweled glass." [4]

The ethereal proportions of this mystical effect are seen expanded in this concentrated (though abridged) quotation from *The Gothic Cathedral: Origins of Gothic Architecture and the Medieval Concept of Order*, by another relatively modern writer, Otto von Simson:

> The Gothic wall seems to be porous: light filters through it, permeating it, merging with it, transfiguring it. The stained-glass windows of the Gothic are structurally and aesthetically not openings in the wall to admit light, but transparent walls. The Gothic may be described as

transparent, diaphanous architecture…a continuous sphere of light. [5]

But however striking such descriptions may appear, the synchronized experience of light and revelation within art is problematic, since it is subjective on so many different levels. For example, a work of art may seem to have an inconsistent brightness or thematic relevance, depending on one's mood, health, focus, or for other reasons. Moreover, such a spirituality contains some other limitations, unique to its foundation.

For example, it is probably most applicable within the fields of cinema, photography, and painting, while being much less applicable to music and to poetry, since these media contain no optical component. In addition, spiritual analogies involving light may not apply in all the Church. However, for individuals--regardless of their culture--with whom this model resonates, these are not concerns. From here, the search for this exciting element within a work of art is simple and rewarding.

I have found that searching for the holy presence via this approach is not at all restricted to the world of so-called high or classical aesthetics (though I find the ideal synthesis of light and scripture content in the work of high medieval painters, who fused the major Christian themes with luminescent color[6]). I suggest that readers watch (or re-examine) movies like *The Sound of Music*, *Howard's End*, and other films, from this unique perspective.

Even so, if such an element is found through holy intuition, the work of some musicians cannot be discounted. Of course, the problem of assigning light and spiritual integrity to art that is invisible, and that often has no storyline, cannot be overstated. However, some works mirror qualities that many people would associate with light, such as major chords and keys, trumpets, harp, sheer and effervescent melodies.

Music of the Church, such as sacred choral chants, must surely fit the bill, as might certain works of Brahms, Vivaldi, Bach, and Mozart; and many of these latter even have religious themes and storylines. Pieces filled with minor chords and keys, and having

ANTHONY BIALOBRYSKI

secular libretti, such as some of Richard Wagner's darker works, might not be the best examples of this form; indeed, such music might have more in common with the most daimonic rockers of our age.

Poetry, and writing overall, is equally subjective. Like music, it contains no optical component, and will often have no Christian or religious theme at all. Still, it is more readily employable in liturgy than are a range of other media. It is also most impressive. One need only sample work by poets such as G.M. Hopkins and A.E. Housman to get glimpses of an imagery infused with crystalline perfection and a corresponding reverence for light in God's creation.

One lyric poem by Housman is a fine example of this genre (and may be useful in retreat or in our personal devotions, perhaps at Easter or at Christmas, or in our contemplation of the Christian year). It is not a whole poem, but part two of a poem entitled "1887," although it has come to be best known as "Loveliest of Trees":

>Loveliest of trees, the cherry now
>Is hung with bloom along the bough,
>And stands about the woodland ride
>Wearing white for Eastertide.
>
>Now of my threescore years and ten,
>Twenty will not come again,
>And take from seventy springs a score,
>It leaves me only fifty more.
>
>And since to look at things in bloom
>Fifty springs are little room,
>About the woodlands I will go
>To see the cherry hung with snow. [7]

Another good example of this element in verse, which may also have some spiritual utility (possibly during times of natural disaster), might be this colorful and striking excerpt from the Robert Frost poem "Birches," which displays the beauty of an otherwise destructive winter ice storm:

Often you must have seen them
Loaded with ice a sunny winter morning
After a rain. They click upon themselves
As the breeze rises, and turn many-colored
As the stir cracks and crazes their enamel.
Soon the sun's warmth makes them shed crystal shells
Shattering and avalanching on the snow-crust[8]

Synthesizing beauty with the fiber of the text conveys my own experience, and allows me to display, up front, such evidence of God embedded in our culture. It also drives a somewhat more ambitious hope, that in reading through these literary sketches on your own, the meaning of the text will be *experienced*. This may be what Catholic theologian Hans Urs von Balthasar was referring to when he said that "a theology of beauty may be elaborated in a beautiful manner" and that "the particular nature of one's subject-matter must first of all be reflected in the particular nature of one's method." [9]

The language of aesthetics is appropriate for spiritual expression and critique. The language of empiricism, while able to explain the workings of creation (in limited detail), projects upon our God the image of an engineer. The language of aesthetics speaks, via our imagination, to the very heart of God, who, if creation will be honestly appraised, ought to be regarded not simply as mechanically inclined, but also as artistic.

This dimension of our God is manifested through the Church-- *and* secular humanity. It is through this creativity that God's identity and presence is more fairly ascertained--as masterful technician *and* as artist. Indeed, the language of aesthetics is perhaps the better means to represent the presence of what von Balthasar referred to as "this single light which transcends all plurality." [10]

Notes

1. Tuan, Yi-Fu. *Passing Strange and Wonderful.* (Covelo, California: Island Press, 1993), pp. 138-139.
2. Ibid., p. 141.
3. Panofsky, Erwin. *Abbot Suger on the Abbey Church of St.-Denis and Its Art Treasures.* (Princeton: Princeton University Press, 1946), pp. 63, 65.
4. Prentice, Sartell. *The Heritage of the Cathedral.* (New York: William Morrow & Co., 1936), p. 170.
5. Simson, von Otto. *The Gothic Cathedral: Origins of Gothic Architecture and the Medieval Concept of Order.* (New York: Pantheon Books, 1962), pp. 3-4.
6. Eco, Umberto. *Art and Beauty in the Middle Ages.* Trans. Hugh Bredin. (New Haven: Yale University Press, 1986), pp. 44-46.
7. Housman, A.E. *The Collected Poems of A.E. Housman.* (New York: Henry Holt and Co., 1940), p. 11.
8. Frost, Robert. *Complete Poems of Robert Frost.* (New York: Holt, Rinehart and Winston, 1961), p. 152.
9. Balthasar, von Hans Urs. *The Glory of the Lord.* Vol. 1. Trans. Erasmo Leiva-Merikakis. Ed. Joseph Fessio and John Riches. (Edinburgh: T. & T. Clark, 1982), p. 39.
10. Balthasar, von Hans Urs. *The Glory of the Lord.* Vol. 2. Trans. Andrew Louth, Francis McDonagh, and Brian McNeil. Ed. John Riches (San Francisco: Ignatius Press, New York: Crossroad, 1984), p. 98.

Chapter 1: The Imagery of Advent

The liturgical year begins amid the glitter-wrap and tinsel of the retail Christmas season. It also coincides with what the mass of people call the start of winter weather. At this time, persons living in the northern climes who rise before the dawn may see what I have called a subtle metaphor for Advent, and for the promise of the seasons that will follow.

On December mornings, before me I have seen the ground effuse with subtle glow: the faint, delicate pink of predawn Advent snow. Lit with rose, and turning slowly crimson in the angled rays of dawn, the world seems cleansed of all defect, of litter and of grime, depravity of sin. By noon the world is sparkling white. Immaculate! Such imagery has given me a vision for the Christian year: for the beauties of reflected light, the cold epiphanies of awe, the treasure of austerity, the sufficiency of sacrifice, the idylls of our ordinary time.

This season of the Christian year has its roots in nature. In the pagan holiday *adventus* it was believed the patron god arrived in manifested form to live within the temple. To celebrate, the priests would open up the temple doors (which normally were closed) and bring the statue of the god into the larger space, for greater adoration.

In a dual context, the feast of adventus celebrated also the coming of the emperor to power--the advent of his reign. As paganism faded, the Christianizing of this feast became a simple matter; the deity descending to the earth became the Christ. Eventually, the feast of Advent came to be a recognition not only of the birth of Christ, but of his *second* coming, and his reign.

But, in the early years of Advent, Christian celebrations of this season were not uniform. In Gaul and Spain, the feast resembled something more like Lent, a time of preparation, but for the incarnation. Advent season came to Rome around the year 550. Unlike in Gaul and Spain, asceticism played no role in Rome's interpretation, which was, at least initially, more liturgically determined. Moreover, it was there that Jesus' second coming became linked to Advent season. In the Byzantine communities, the emphasis was on, and remains on, the *mystery* of Jesus' incarnation. Their celebration seems the antithesis of Lent. Indeed, this use of "celebration" is precise, for their worship at this time is often filled with partying and dance.

The Advent season of today, so closely tied to Christmas, does not mirror celebrations held in early Christian Gaul or Spain. Quite the contrary! The Advent of the Christian year seems more a signal of the pagan feast adventus than of the coming of our Lord. Perhaps the happy medium *is* found in Orthodox traditions, with their lively celebrations that retain the meaning and the destination of this season.

The Advent celebration intimates a complementarity of time. It inaugurates the Christian year, yet shifts our focus to the final things of Christian eschatology; fusing both the joy of Christmas and the message of Ash Wednesday, it is the mirror complement to Lent. This complementarity exists on yet another level--for as the Christian year begins, the civil year declines. The calendars exist in parallel alignment, reflecting contradictions, and yet, each other.

The impetus of Advent beckons us toward springtime, toward Easter, and a greater comprehension of atonement. It gives us also vision for the end of time, nurturing a hushed anticipation that "All shall be well"--while reminding us that it is early. This unlikely harmony pervades our Christian liturgy, devotions, and the arts. In "Little Gidding," T.S. Eliot proclaims: "What we call the beginning is often the end/And to make an end is to make a beginning./The end is where we start from."[1] Eliot continues: "We shall not cease from exploration/And the end of all our exploring/Will be to arrive where we started/And know the place for the first time."[2]

The impetus of Advent is revealed in God's creation: in the slanted light of fading afternoon; in the hours after midnight--the springtime constellations tangled low in branches; and in the granule frostwork of the dawn. The impetus of Advent moves us toward the apex of the Christian year, while foreshadowing its end. In offering the Christian faith this comprehensive view, the imagery of Advent intimates divine perspective--timelessness--revealed through human symbol: the language and the imagery of time.

Notes

1. Eliot, T. S. *The Complete Poems and Plays 1909-1950.* (New York: Harcourt, Brace & World, 1952), p. 144.
2. Ibid., p. 145.

Chapter 2: The Imagery of Christmastime

We see it in the flashy wrapping of our gifts; in windows strung with colored lights--the glow of emerald, ruby, and electric blue; in the momentary glint of tinsel; and in the brightest star. Perhaps no season of the year is more imbued with holy light than that of Christmastime, yet few of us can see the light of God within the glitz.

Some Christians call its imagery a crass, commercial lie. Some reject it all as pagan. Others are combative--the holiday was even banned![1] But for many Christians in the world, its roots are holy, begun anew, atop its pagan imagery. This imagery can intimate the majesty of light that pierced the skies of Bethlehem, the huddled glow that filled the faces of the Magi in the night.

And yet, the imagery of Christmas seems so closely tied to nature that it gives us pause. This imagery seems often to resemble less the symbols of our Christian faith, and more a winter festival. In his short piece, entitled simply "Christmas," the nineteenth-century American writer Washington Irving recalls, albeit naively, the imagery of Christmas past:

> The old halls of castles and manor houses resounded with the harp and the Christmas carol, and their ample boards groaned under the weight of hospitality. Even the poorest cottage welcomed the festive season with green decorations of bay and holly--the cheerful fire glanced its rays through the lattice, inviting the passenger to raise the latch.[2]

The poor of any time or place might deem this view naïvely (if not grotesquely) imprecise. But this view reflects as well a point of irony: that community and charity, elusive in the Church at other times, abound amid the shimmering light of tinsel; that Jesus' call to feed the poor is heeded best amid the ornamented boughs and fragrance of a cut green tree.

The feast of the nativity has clearly pagan roots within the celebration *sol invictus* or "invincible sun." Instituted by Aurelius in 274 A.D., and celebrated on December 25th, it marked the slow return of light beyond the winter solstice. A Christian version of this feast, observed in Egypt and Arabia, on January 6th, became the feast of Christ's nativity. This feast was named Epiphany. For pagans, newly Christianized, it was easy to accept the altered meaning of these feasts, because the scriptures use the sun and light as metaphors for Christ.

For example, in Malachi 4:2 we read: "But for you who revere my name, the sun of righteousness will rise with healing in its wings" (NIV); moreover, John refers to Jesus constantly as light. In John 8:12 Christ himself proclaims, "I am the Light of the world" (NIV). In time, this feast of Christ's nativity was changed in *name*--to Christmas. Epiphany was changed, in *theme*, from the manifestation of Jesus' incarnation, to that of his divinity. Gradually, Christ became the sol invictus, having vanquished *inner* darkness and its power to control us.

This connection of the seasons to the human soul is not at all surprising. Perception of the world may ebb and flow with weather or the seasons. This shift is seen in melancholy brought on by the winter weather, particularly by its muted light. Those who suffer from this winter gloom internalize the darkened world, allowing it to shape their mood and outlook on reality. The presence of this parallel, in ancient and medieval times, may have been pronounced--even more so than today. It is not unreasonable to see the dimness of that pre-electric world, combined with a collapsing (if not an utterly collapsed) society, as having greatly shaped the nature of our faith.

For this reason, it may be right to argue for the worth of Christmas imagery today, if for nothing else than as a form of therapy. Its value, up or down, is really just a matter of perception. All that may be needed is a healthy vision of its place in Christian life. With such a view, the festive wrapping of our presents may remind us not of retail profits, but of the Magi's precious offerings to Christ; and perhaps the glow of Christmas lights might come to seem like stones from New Jerusalem. The premise of this view might be that God remains inherent in creation, despite the human fall--that evidence of God is stored within its elemental structure.

Such a view is hardly innovative; rather, it is just a variation of medieval Catholic thinking. In medieval Europe, one person who articulated this theology was Bonaventure. He observed that transparent windowpanes are created out of sand and ashes, that fire results from striking coal, and that precious stones and metals shine when they are polished.[3] Yi-Fu Tuan writes:

> Even gross matter, since it was God's creation, must contain light, however dim. Among material substances, jewels occupied a privileged position. Medieval jewels were not faceted, as was the custom during the Renaissance, but were rounded and polished so as to give an impression of light glowing from within.[4]

The colors of the Christmas season glow like jewels against the night. They give us pause to look behind, to Bethlehem, and on with expectation to the heavenly New Jerusalem. The luster of Epiphany sustains the joy of Christmastide--beyond the time allotted us by secular tradition. Similar to Advent, the imagery of Christmas beckons to the Christian mind a vantage of eternity, of timelessness. In liturgy this imagery evokes more readily the glory of that wondrous night--the splendor of that awesome sky, the star of promise burning clear.

Notes

1. "The Puritans made such a fierce assault upon the ceremonies of the church, and poor old Christmas was driven out of the land by proclamation of Parliament... [Footnote] From the "Flying Eagle," a small Gazette published December 24th, 1652.--'The House spent much time this day about the businesse of the Navy for settling the affairs at sea, and before they rose were presented with a terrible remonstrance against Christmas day, grounded upon divine Scriptures... In which Christmas is called Antichrist's masse, and those Masse-mongers and Papists who observe it, & c. In consequence of which Parliament spent some time in consultation about the abolition of Christmas day, passed orders to that effect, and resolved to sit on the following day, which was commonly called Christmas day.'" See *The Complete Works of Washington Irving.* Vol. 8. Ed. Haskell Springer (Boston: Twayne Publishers, 1978), pp. 175-176.

2. Ibid., p. 150.

3. Simson von Otto. *The Gothic Cathedral: Origins of Gothic Architecture and the Medieval Concept of Order.* (New York: Pantheon Books, 1962), pp. 51-52.

4. *Passing Strange and Wonderful: Aesthetics, Nature, and Culture.* (Washington, DC: Island Press, 1993), p. 139.

Chapter 3: Memories of an Epiphany

In February of 1977, I had just moved from New York to the relatively tropical climate of northeast Florida, and was living in the generally wooded area of Jacksonville between the beach and town. It is, as I remember it, a curious topography, a zone of seemingly contradictory but harmonic contrasts: a blend of desert, deciduous forest and swamp, where, in autumn, white sand is blown against trees lit with foliage of orange, burnt copper, and red. Here, in a secluded neighborhood, I had rented a small house adjacent to an open field that was covered with white sand, nettles, and grass.

In spring, and especially in the summertime, this land evoked for me the imagery of Israel found in scripture (northeast Florida and Israel are on roughly the same latitude). I recognized the parallels between these worlds from reading Isaiah. In Isaiah 41:19 (NIV) we read: "I will set pines in the wasteland, the fir and the cypress together." Since then, I have likely idealized the memory of this topography, and as a consequence, I have likely also morphed this memory with visions of an ancient Palestine that never did exist. Consequently, much of Isaiah supplies me with glimpses of landscapes grown sacred with time.

The winter of 1977-78 revealed to me at once the nature of this world, upon arrival of the first cold weather, and, of all things, snow! As a native New Yorker, I had always been led to believe that the climate of Florida was similar to that of St. Tropez or Maui. I discovered in time that the northeastern corner of Florida boasted a climate akin to the mid-south of France, and so, was annually subjected to subfreezing temperatures, though rarely if ever to snow.

ANTHONY BIALOBRYSKI

Fire and Ice

The morning of January 6th, 1978 was surprisingly warm, compared to the weather the morning before, and blindingly sunny. Wispy filaments of cirrus hung suspended near the zenith of the sky, but provided no obstruction to the dazzling effulgence that flooded the world outside of my door. In many ways, the atmosphere that winter morning mirrored the topography below, as both exuded an unearthly synthesis of opposites. In this curious world of palm trees, palmetto, and pinecones, that atmosphere struck me as alien, albeit invigoratingly so, an austere fusion of pristinely frigid air and blinding sun.

It was an experience that bore a striking, if imperfect, resemblance to the opening lines of T.S. Eliot's poem "Little Gidding" (named for the town in England), when he writes, "Midwinter spring is its own season... Suspended in time, between pole and tropic." He continues:

When the short day is brightest, with frost and fire,
The brief sun flames the ice, on pond and ditches,
In windless cold that is the heart's heat,
Reflecting in a watery mirror
A glare that is blindness in the early afternoon.
And glow more intense than blaze of branch, or brazier,
Stirs the dumb spirit: no wind, but pentecostal fire...[1]

This allusion by Eliot to the complementary relation of our spirit and senses, condensed in the metaphor of fire, conveys also the simultaneous experience of spiritual and optic revelation. In a sense, this fusion is the basis of the Christian celebration of Epiphany. For it was only when the Magi *looked* upon the world's messiah that they were to realize his divinity.

Now, while we may not have been party to that first Epiphany, we may still observe the fruit of God's creative power and, perhaps, receive some revelation in that observation. This is what occurred for

26

me that brilliant winter day, as I stood outside, behind my little rented house. It was a simple revelation that accompanied my sense of God amid the dazzling sunlight. What facilitated this most simple revelation was what seemed to me to be the *actual* experience of spring. With modulated temperature (and temporary blindness) came emotions, memories, and realizations that normally resurface in the early spring and during Easter. It would not be a stretch for me to say it felt more like the spring than did the spring, and that in this I experienced the presence of our God more deeply than I ever have before. The revelation was a colorful reminder that the theme of resurrection is a major, if not the ultimate, defining theme of God's creation, and that it recurs in the inner and external aspects of our temporal existence, in the spiritual and in the physical, in the personal and in the natural domain.

In *The Practice of the Presence of God*, the seventeenth-century Discalced Carmelite monk Nicholas Herman, otherwise known as Brother Laurence of the Resurrection, recounts something of a similar experience. While not rendered via striking imagery, this description intimates that his experience was, in its way, profoundly visual:

> He said that, one winter day as he was looking at a tree stripped of its leaves and considering that sometime later these leaves would appear again, then flowers, then fruits, he received a profound impression of the providence and the power of God, which was never effaced from his soul. He declared that this impression detatched him entirely from the world and gave him such a love of God that he could not say whether it had ever increased in the more than forty years since he had received this grace. [2]

Conclusions

Observance of the Christian year sustains our sense of continuity. This observance is a form of nourishment reminding us not only of God's sovereignty, but of his constancy, through all seasons of this temporal existence. Spring is, in itself, a perennial expression of this message. Quoting the *New York Times* editorial writer, Hal Borland, in *Liturgical Spirituality*, Philip Pfatteicher writes: "We are sustained by the certainty 'that no matter how cold or bitter the winter, there will be violets again... that spring will follow winter.'" [3] Borland even goes so far as intimating that the ultimate necessity of having to experience the bitterness of winter may be, in itself, evidence of God:

> Maybe we need to learn these things anew each year. Perhaps we need to face the snowstorm and feel the frost underfoot to know that there is both ice and fire in earth, even as in the stars; to know that the big assurances endure.[4]

The grandest of all reassurances was granted to me that day, some twenty-six years ago, through the experience of nature. It was in that vision that I saw, and still see, fulfillment of God's faithfulness and sovereignty. In retrospect, I occasionally long to see again the curious topography around that little rented house in Jacksonville, Florida. I long to see it as I remember it--landscape strewn with pine trees, palmetto, and palm branches, the sacred field dazzling in ice beneath the tropical sun. I would look out over those immaculate acres and I would recall the words of Isaiah 35:1-2 (NIV): "The wilderness will rejoice and blossom. Like the crocus, it will burst into bloom."

Notes

1. Eliot, T. S. *The Complete Poems and Plays 1909-1950.* (New York: Harcourt, Brace & World, 1952), p. 138.
2. Brother Lawrence. *The Practice of the Presence of God.* Trans. Mary David (Westminster, Maryland: The Newman Book Shop, 1945), p. 63.
3. Borland, Hal & Pfatteicher, Philip H. Quoted in *Liturgical Spirituality.* (Valley Forge, Pennsylvania: Trinity Press International, 1997), p. 106.
4. Ibid., p. 106.

Chapter 4: The Weeks Beyond Epiphany

The weeks beyond Epiphany are, for many, the least discovered part of Ordinary Time. This segment of the calendar can be a chance to pause and rest, *from* the lengthy Christmas season--and *for* the challenge just ahead. It serves also to buffer our withdrawal from the season's frantic pace, allowing us to taste again the sense of normalcy in life. It can also be a time for us to taste again the sense of what is special in our "ordinary" time. But perhaps its greatest value lies within its graduated theme,[1] allowing us to "ramp down" from the holidays, thus *phasing* in the muted tones of Lent.

In the cold of January, time appears suspended; yet nature, and the Church, are very much alive. In both these realms the hand of God reveals, through subtle imagery, unique perspective via scripture and the hope of promised resurrection. In his poem "Ice," Charles G.D. Roberts writes:

> When Winter scourged the meadow and the hill
> And in the withered leafage worked his will,
> The water shrank, and shuddered, and stood still,--
> Then built himself a magic house of glass,
> Irised with memories of flowers and grass,
> Wherein to sit and watch the fury pass.[2]

However, in the dark and sometimes unrelenting cold of January days, we come the closest that we may to "after-Christmas blues." But this time affords the Church a chance to tap into itself; for in the house of fellowship we find our insulation. Even hermits come to pray. Safe within our father's house, inside its walls of colored glass, the Christian finds his rest. Within the church itself, this promise is reflected in the vestment of the priest. The color of this vestment (green) evokes the resurrection, infuses life into the air of Ordinary Time.

Come February 2nd, we see some further hints of spring, of Easter, and of the growing light. The "Presentation of the Lord," known to some as "Candlemas," beckons to Epiphany, but still contains a subtle paschal theme. This solemnity marks the day of Jesus' dedication at the temple, with a candlelit procession and a liturgy of light:

> God our Father, source of eternal light,
> fill the hearts of all believers
> with the light of faith.
> May we who carry these candles in your church
> come with joy to the light of glory.[3]

The days between Epiphany and Lent are filled with life, waiting to be stirred, as sleeping in the frozen earth resides the spring, waiting for the breath of God to call it forth. Within the Church, the weeks beyond Epiphany are times not only for our rest, but for our application. The liturgy of Christmas season occupied our focus and our hands. Now our minds and hands are free; it is now that Christians may employ the lessons learned.

In Ecclesiastes 9:7 we read that "it is now that God favors what you do" (NIV). Beneath our winter moods and slumber lies the essence of this time, if only we will notice. In another poem, "The Brook in February," Charles G.D. Roberts writes: "But low, bend low a listening ear!/Beneath the mask of moveless white/A babbling whisper you shall hear/Of birds and blossoms, leaves and light." [4]

Notes

1. The theme of Christ's nativity continues in degrees even into Ordinary Time.

2. *The Oxford Book of Canadian Verse.* Ed. A. J. M. Smith. (Toronto: Oxford University Press, 1960), p. 71. Hereafter referred to as *Oxford.*

3. *Days of the Lord: The Liturgical Year.* Vol. 7. Trans. M. Beaumont & M. Misrahi (Collegeville, Minnesota: The Liturgical Press, 1994), p. 104.

4. *Oxford*, p. 71.

Chapter 5: The Cold Cheer of Lent

As February steadily unfolds, we begin to change the focus of our spiritual direction, from retrospective to the future: from that of Christmas, and of winter, to the grand crescendo of the Christian year, Easter, and the coming of the spring. The initial signpost of this seasonal transition, Ash Wednesday--the "porch" of what we know as Lent--has now arrived.

Initial references to Lent would indicate its origin as being somewhere near the year 300, although the nature of this season has evolved since then, passing through a series of adjustments. The first extended several centuries (from the fourth until, possibly, the twelfth). The second phase, of similar duration, and in which the season was to stay essentially unchanged, lasted till the early nineteen sixties; and a third began a few years later with the papal promulgation of the Missal, the Lectionary, and the Roman Calendar.

Lent has had an inconsistent image in both popular and educated minds. Some consider it a pointless, if not unhealthy, artifact of early Christian culture, utterly removed from modern place and time. This is understandable, as many in contemporary culture, including many in the Church, seem to have diminished interest in ascetical concerns.

The movie *Chocolat* presents this adverse view of Lent. The plot is set within a small French town, and revolves around a staunchly Catholic (and unhappy) mayor, determined to enforce his austere lifestyle on the local people. When a pretty, single woman opens up a chocolate shop in town, he meets her and discovers that she does not go to church. Incensed enough at this, he fumes at learning that she plans to open up her chocolate business in "the Lenten fast." He embarks upon a personal crusade to drive her from the village, employing ugly tactics, such as spreading rumors--that she is an atheist, and eventually, that she killed a woman in the town.

For some, however (including, it is to be hoped, the majority of Catholics), Lent presents a chance for introspection, inventory, repentance, and of measured self-denial, a period of appropriate and *joyous* sobriety--what Marie Borroff, in her rendering of *Sir Gawain and the Green Knight*, translates as "the cold cheer of Lent"--[1] but which also, as W.R.J. Barron continues in his own translation, "tries the flesh with its fish and plainer fare."[2] And so, despite this element of joy, the sensual component of the season remains muted.

Even in our time, this is evidenced in modulated diet, and in some churches, the covering of statues, pictures and other church adornments--temporarily. A passage in *Days of the Lord: The Liturgical Year* reveals the optimistic forethought and incentive for this tenor:

> If the Church refrains from singing Alleluia during this whole time, it is not to have us robed in sadness, but to deepen our joy and to cause the Resurrection Alleluia to burst out more vibrantly and endlessly reverberate from one assembly to another to the four corners of the world on the night when Christ appears bathed in light.[3]

Despite this focus on the testing and refining of the self, the Lenten season is not meant to be a time of personal withdrawal, but rather, one of personal encounter, shared within the Church, for the benefit of all. This perspective underlies the Christian church tradition. For instance, as far back as 130 A.D., in the *Didaskalia Apostolorum* ("Teaching of the Apostles"), we read that "When there are poor persons among them needing help, Christians fast for two or three days and customarily send them the food that they had prepared for themselves."[4]

In the volume of *The Liturgy of the Hours* devoted to the Lenten season, we are reminded that such acts of charity are giving to the

Lord himself; self-denial for the benefit of others is explained to be a means of showing gratitude to God. Saint Gregory of Nazianzen writes:

> What benefactor has enabled you to look out upon the beauty of the sky, the sun in its course, the circle of the moon, the countless numbers of stars, with the harmony and order that are theirs, like the music of a harp? Who has blessed you with rain, with the art of husbandry, with different kinds of food, with the arts, with houses… with a life of humanity and culture…will we not be ashamed to refuse him this one thing only, our generosity? [5]

This focus on the point of fasting cues us that this season is a time of cleansing, in preparation for the Easter celebration. This cleansing of the Church begins while on the porch of Lent, in its observation of Ash Wednesday, a day whose very name evokes the scriptural reminder given by the Lord to Adam and his lineage: "Dust you are, and to dust you will return."

The use of ashes is related to this act of cleansing, as ashes were employed by many ancient peoples as a form of cleanser, and also as they (ashes) symbolize the inner cleansing of repentance. Their use imbues the Lenten season with appropriate perspective, calling us to soberly reflect upon the way we live our lives, and its possible effect upon our ultimate condition. In this way, Ash Wednesday calls us to observe our need for cleansing through the cross, and for our faithful stewardship of such a precious gift.

This reminder is developed in the Lenten scripture text, particularly concerning Israel's desert trek. This text reveals the parallel between the Sinai congregation and the future, Christian church. Such a parallel is evident not only in the Israelites' encounter with their sins, but also in their regimen of manna. We might consider Israel's trek as not unlike a much extended Lent, a cleansing of God's people--but lasting forty *years*--instead of days.

This dynamic of renewal is also evident in nature, in the thaw that invariably occurs within the Lenten season. The melting ice and snow may also signal our arrival in the promised land of spring. In this way we may observe this process as occurring inwardly *and* in the outer world. In the writings of the naturalist Thoreau we see a vivid picture of this metaphor at work:

> The change from storm and winter to serene and mild weather, from dark and sluggish hours to bright and elastic ones, is a memorable crisis which all things proclaim. It is seemingly instantaneous at last. Suddenly an influx of light filled my house, though the evening was at hand, and the clouds of winter still overhung it, and the eaves were dripping with sleety rain. I looked out the window, and lo! where yesterday was cold gray ice there lay the transparent pond already calm and full of hope as in a summer evening, reflecting a summer evening sky in its bosom. The pitch-pines and shrub-oaks about my house, which had so long drooped, suddenly resumed their several characters, looked brighter, greener, and more erect and alive, as if effectively cleansed and restored by the rain.[6]

Lent imparts a bracing air to Christian time and liturgy. It gives communities of faith a stark but edifying glimpse into the choice continually before them, that of growth or of stagnation. Such bearing on our spiritual direction may not be as evident at Christmastime or Easter, when we are flooded with distractions. For this and other reasons, many have suggested Lent to be the more appropriate beginning for the Christian year.

Finally, the Lenten season is a chance for Catholics to explore the value of asceticism for themselves. Some may not feel called to exercise this option, in any form at all; others may consider only minimal restrictions. Some may set exemplary examples, and *need* no extra discipline. But in cultures like our own, bent on excess and indulgence, such individuals are likely a minority. For most of us within the Church, *some* degree of discipline is worth consideration. In the end, we may discover that the Lenten fast is but a chance to, in the words of St. Ireneus, "Become what you are."

Notes

1. Published by W.W. Norton & Co., 2001, p. 27.
2. Published by Manchester University Press, 1974, p. 55.
3. *Days of the Lord: The Liturgical Year.* Vol. 2. Trans. Madeleine Beaumont (Collegeville, Minnesota: The Liturgical Press, 1993), p. 12.
4. *Didaskalia Apostolorum,* 1:5.
5. Vol. 2. (New York: Catholic Book Publishing Co., 1976), pp. 96-97.
6. *Walden.* (New York: Book of the Month Club, 1996), pp. 412-413.

Chapter 6: The Imagery of Easter

With the Lenten chill subsided, the sodden earth awakens in the sun. The purity of spring imbues the world with hopeful expectation. Dandelions tatter the lawn; a sweet bouquet of lilac fills the air; oak and maple branches flourish, and cherry trees are cluttered with white blossoms. In this season of the Christian year, the world seems doubly renewed. The worlds of nature and the Church appear to be in harmony. "The spring, nature's resurrection, is both a symbol of Christ's resurrection and nature's way of greeting the risen Lord. It is as if nature can not help but join in the praise and the greeting of that morning that transformed the world and all that is in it."[1]

Though Lent fades almost imperceptibly, its formal end arrives the Thursday night preceding Easter Sunday. However, in a curious division of that pivotal day, its morning and the afternoon still belong to Lent. And even though the final service of that season, the Chrism Mass, occurs that morning, its liturgy contains no *clearly* Lenten theme; nor does it speak of Easter (although it does direct attention to the paschal character of baptism, confirmation, ordination, and the anointing of the sick). The Mass concludes, gives way to afternoon, anticipation of the sunset, and eventually, to the very seam of dusk and evening, that "intersection of the timeless moment"[2] neither Lent nor Easter, light nor dark.

Hushed in celebration, the people filter into church. Now, on Holy Thursday, the evening Mass begins. On other, less important nights, this Mass might seem, in a word, ordinary--even unremarkable to some. In truth of fact, the Mass of The Lord's Supper can almost seem a Mass from Ordinary Time. What elevates *this* night? The intersecting lines of theme and time. On this special night, the Eucharist may seem most concentrated: communion perfected, of purpose and of instance, of Deity and Church. In time, the service comes to closure, concluding in procession to the place of Eucharistic reservation, preserved until the morrow. In a profoundly potent and unsettling action, the altar is stripped. The building darkened, the people of God exit in silence.

On the morning of Good Friday, anticipation grows. The celebration of this day combines the Liturgy of the Word, the Veneration of the Cross, and the Holy Eucharist. It is not a day of darkness or grief, despite the muted tones. The painted illustration in the *Belles Heures of Jean, Duke of Berry* depicts the day as solemn. We see the crucifixion scene against a somber backdrop--an overcast Judean sky.[3] The theme is awe in manifold dimensions: hearts fail; nature reverberates. The artist shows the cosmic scope in shades of murky light, evocative of Sheol. Against this stark milieu the drama of the cross emerges, more vivid in the darkness:

> Behold the tree of life
> where the light of the world shines in the darkness
> to accomplish the Passover of the universe.[4]

On Holy Saturday we begin our wait in earnest for the Sunday dawn, and contemplate the Lord's descent to hell. In *The Liturgy of the Hours* we read:

Something strange is happening--there is a great silence on earth today, a great silence and stillness. The whole earth keeps silence because the King is asleep. The earth trembled and is still because God has fallen asleep in the flesh and he has raised up all who have slept ever since the world began. God has died in the flesh and hell trembles with fear. He has gone to search for our first parent, as for a lost sheep. Greatly desiring to visit those who live in darkness and in the shadow of death, he has gone to free from sorrow the captives Adam and Eve.[5]

The Easter Vigil starts that evening, after Vespers, with the blessing of the fire. With the lighting and procession of the Easter candle comes the *Exsultet*. Soon the church interior is glowing, incandescent with emotion. Soon thereafter come the Liturgy of the Word, the Liturgy of Baptism, and finally, the Eucharistic liturgy. On this night the majesty of Easter is displayed; the resurrection of our nature, taking place with nature, is nearing its completion:

> O night sweeter than heaven
> Night of wakefulness for all the Body
> Night when the breath fills the earth
> Night that glitters with light...
> Night of living water after the frost. [6]

On Easter Sunday morning, light pervades the church: assorted flowers and bouquets--daisies, violets, roses in the snow of baby's breath--colored ribbons, and stained glass windows lit with imagery. The atmosphere today is festive, yet majestic. In bursts of Alleluias, the congregation celebrates the news of resurrection. The Easter hymn *Salve, festa dies* hails this restoration:

> Earth her joy confesses, clothing her for spring,
> All fresh gifts return with her returning King:
> Bloom in every meadow, leaves on every bough,
> Speak his sorrow ended, hail his triumph now. [7]

Easter Sunday liturgy, no less regal than the Vigil's, exudes a satisfaction. It is more relaxed, and simply worded. To use more complex liturgy would shift our focus from the moment. In this way, the Church both celebrates and *contemplates* the news of resurrection. In time, request is made of God to manifest this work within the Church. Later, the Triduum is drawn to its conclusion with the Easter evening office--and yet, in terms of Christian time, the Easter celebration is only now beginning. For although the Easter Triduum lasts from Holy Thursday until Sunday's evening office,

Easter season stretches on to Pentecost--in duration second only to the span of Ordinary Time. And unlike Lent, the days that follow Easter Sunday do not constitute a preparation, but rather, an extension of a celebration. This is reflected in *The Liturgy of the Hours*, which regards these not as Sundays *after* Easter, but as Sundays *of* it.

April fades to May, and the smell of rain foreshadows summer latitude. In these Sundays nature's bloom is in fruition. Easter season also brings a ripened tone in liturgy. Details of the paschal theme are given sharper focus, creating in the Church the hope of growth. Maturity is seen in various dimensions--personal, collective, and in our contact with the secular community. In *Days of the Lord: The Liturgical Year*, this dimension is revealed within the context of community:

> In these Easter days,
> Lord God,
> your vine receives new sap.
> Hold the branches to the vine:
> thus will charity make us live
> one for another
> in the one who died and rose for us.[8]

Nature's imagery proclaims the news of resurrection, our own, of our Lord, and of all creation, in holy synchronicity. Scripture itself declares, "By him are all things held together." Pierre Teilhard de Chardin writes: "Whoever will passionately love Jesus, hidden in the forces that make the earth grow, him the earth will lift up, like a mother in her huge arms, and allow him to contemplate the face of God."[9] Easter's living imagery proclaims that face in sweet and subtle ways: the glitter-wrap of chocolate eggs on green confetti grass, the flashy violet of crocus, the snowy pink of cherry blossoms carpeting our parish. In a myriad of other ways--sculpture, stained glass, liturgy, and song--the imagery of nature both fills and guides the paschal celebration.

Notes

1. Pfatteicher, Philip H. *Liturgical Spirituality*. (Valley Forge, Pennsylvania: Trinity Press International, 1997), p. 77. Hereafter referred to as *Liturgical*.
2. Eliot, T.S. *The Complete Poems and Plays 1909-1950*. (New York: Harcourt, Brace & World, 1952), p. 138.
3. *The Belles Heures of Jean, Duke of Berry Prince of France*. (New York: The Metropolitan Museum of Art, 1958), pp. 11, 29.
4. *Days of the Lord: The Liturgical Year*. Vol. 3. Trans. Greg LaNave & Donald Molloy. (Collegeville, Minnesota: The Liturgical Press, 1993), p. 35. Hereafter referred to as *Days*.
5. *The Liturgy of the Hours*. Vol. 2. (New York: Catholic Book Publishing Co., 1976), pp. 496-497.
6. *Days*, pp. 65-66.
7. *Liturgical*, p. 76.
8. *Days*, p. 169.
9. Ibid., p. 173.

Chapter 7: Life in Ordinary Time

With the conclusion of Pentecost Sunday the Church re-enters what can easily appear to be the most intimidating season in the Christian year, the monolithic and often challenging component of "Ordinary Time." In the early days of its inception, this season's very name wrought great confusion among laity unversed in changes to liturgical vocabulary. Since then, however, ambiguities and fallacies associated with this season have been clarified--though not entirely. Mentioning the imminent arrival of "Ordinary Time" may still evoke a foretaste of the summer doldrums in contemporary Catholics.

For them, this season of the Christian year (particularly the six-month period between Pentecost and Advent) seems to carry all the promise of a prolonged summer drought, with only the hope of heat lightning to punctuate its interminable tedium. In his poem "Gerontion," T.S. Eliot captures something of this mood, writing: "Here I am, an old man in a dry month,/Being read to by a boy, waiting for rain... Signs are taken for wonders. 'We would see a sign!'... Thoughts of a dry brain in a dry season."[1]

Indeed, to the more cynical, this season might appear not merely unremarkable, but evidence that the reformers had exhausted their supply of inspiration or ideas just halfway through the year, or even that they meant this time to be a self-designed vacation for the Church's leadership. Doubtless, some among the laity believe that they are following the Church's lead in taking a more "leisurely" approach to Christian life. Personally, I would suggest that, in this season, it is not the leadership that sets the tone.

This is borne out by the precedence of individual and family vacations in these months--a tradition that, in Europe and America, predates the modern day liturgical reform. These interruptions invariably disrupt the rhythm of the season. Granted, celebrations in this time do not exude the concentrated pageantry or richness of the Easter season or of Christmas, or even the momentum underlying Lent. The few distinctive days within the Spring-Summer-Fall component of Ordinary Time are famously low-key.

This perception of monotony is likely also due, in some part, to the somewhat heavy load of scripture study scheduled for this season--or at least to the *expectation* of having to endure it. But despite the somewhat banal image of this season, it need not be regarded as mundane or "ordinary"--indeed, it must not, if we are to shun the serpent of ingratitude.

This season offers us the opportunity to think creatively and with increased autonomy. For example, during summer Ordinary Time some parishes may have a latitude approximating that of a retreat establishment, offering that parish options for expression and refinement of its own identity. However, this is rarely recognized or understood in full, and so these opportunities are often lost within the haze of summer tedium.

These opportunities may, in fact, be nurtured by this tedium. For example, the prospect of diminished congregation must relieve the Church's hermits, since, with many empty pews, there likely is diminished pressure to participate in fellowship--especially "directed" introductions--in lieu of genuine, spontaneous encounters. Perhaps this factor makes it easier for them to interact with genuine sincerity.

Though the hermit population in the Church amounts to a minority, the lessening of pressure on this group is bound to be significant, for them and others. In this vein, the role of summer travel is a factor, for even hermits will desire *some* variety of venue for their solitude. This change of venue may increase the likelihood of their exploring daily Christian fellowship--in the safety of another faith community. It may be for this reason, among others, that

Ordinary Time (especially in its spring and summer months) emerges as the time of choice for spiritual retreats, away from one's community, in novel, non-demanding venues. So these months of Ordinary Time present some ideal opportunities for welcoming vacationers (hermits or not) to our faith communities. It is an opportunity to cultivate relationships and work on projects with a qualitative view, that might not otherwise be possible outside the setting and relaxed momentum of a summertime vacation. And yet, it is not a time for Catholics to go blindly independent, to forego all instruction, or, as so commonly occurs, all discipline. In this way, Ordinary Time is "the opportunity for us to take our time without wasting it."[2]

We may also find, especially in July and August, that a strong temptation to succumb to lethargy, to linger in our tasks and in our faith, becomes a constant challenge; the very air of summertime creates intoxication. The nineteenth-century American author Washington Irving describes this curious effect, which he encountered in the Catskill Mountains of New York:

There is a little valley, or rather lap of land among high hills, which is one of the quietest places in the whole world. A small brook glides through it, with just murmur enough to lull one to repose, and the occasional whistle of a quail, or tapping of a woodpecker, is almost the only sound that ever breaks in upon the uniform tranquility... If ever I should wish for a retreat, whither I might steal from the world and its distractions, and dream quietly away the remnant of a troubled life, I know of none more promising than this little valley... A drowsy, dreamy influence seems to hang over the land, and to pervade the very atmosphere.[3]

This atmosphere is not unique to any time or place. Here and now it can induce a somnolence akin to Irving's, and with it a delusion able to deceive the holiest among us. It fosters an impression counter to the message of Ash Wednesday--that of human invulnerability and continuity. Hal Borland writes: "Whence comes the boast that man possesses the earth? Summer gives it the lie every hour of the day. Summer proves it, summer, the achievement beyond all human dreams and capacities."⁴ The imagery of Ordinary Time is beautiful, and not at all to be disparaged, shunned, or demonized. But its hauntingly seductive atmosphere can easily exasperate the challenges that face the Church in Ordinary Time, lulling it and fostering complacence.

One may attempt to combat this effect in many different ways. The most effective method that this author has discovered is that of "scripturalizing" summer imagery. If one's neighborhood or church is sited in a rural, a suburban, or even in an urban area, one might easily locate scriptures that describe this area. For example, Isaiah 18:4 reads, "This is what the LORD says to me: I will remain quiet and will look on from my dwelling place, like shimmering heat in the sunshine, like a cloud of dew in the heat of harvest" (NIV). Even relatively barren landscapes may evoke the hope of palpable refreshment, as in Isaiah 43:18-20: "Forget the former things; do not dwell on the past. See, I am doing a new thing! Now it springs up; do you not perceive it? I am making a way in the desert and streams in the wasteland" (NIV).

While nature imagery is likely not accessible to city dwellers (assuming that there is no local park), much of Bible imagery is urban, taking place within Jerusalem or other cityscapes. Such urban imagery need not even seem overtly beautiful for it to be a blessing. In some cases drama can produce a sense of blessing. One has but to read the Book of Lamentations to appreciate potential analogues in housing projects and in slums. By recognizing such potential analogues, it is possible to forge associations with the basis of our faith (scripture) and atmospheres that normally induce the state of lethargy. Hence, when I find such imagery, natural or urban, I focus on the meaning of the scripture that it brings to mind, and so, upon the basis of our faith as it relates to Ordinary Time.

As the Dog Days of August give way to the cooling breezes of September, individuals and families return from their vacations. Work and family routines resume their normal rhythms. Summer's end brings also normalcy of rhythm to the Christian year. Church attendance likely will reflect the gradually returning population, and there is often an exciting newness in the air; friends are reunited, relationships are reaffirmed, and a suddenly renewed appreciation for the church can be experienced. Cherished memories and sweet associations, oftentimes embedded deep within the church's physical construction or in the soft inflections of a voice may re-emerge.

Through late September and October, we may, depending on our latitude, be treated to displays of foliage that are riotous with color. A contemplative's dream, such environments may call us easily to prayer, as we amble in "afternoon light like applesauce spiced with cinnamon."[5] The tempo of the Christian calendar gains palpable momentum as the hint of chill and signs of early frost foreshadow the arrival of the winter and of Advent season.

The opening lines of Margaret Gibson's poem "Long Walks in the Afternoon" convey this sense of mood in living color: "Last night the first light frost, and now sycamore and sumac edge yellow and red in low sun and indian afternoons."[6] Lines from Jody Aliesan's poem "This Fall" illuminate as well the turning of the season: "this fall the japanese maple turned coral red/last fall it turned the color of pumpkins."[7] In these final Sundays after Pentecost, the Church begins to feel the tug of this transition and a sharpening of focus. As November draws to a conclusion, the place of Ordinary Time within the Christian year becomes more evident.

Ordinary Time is not mere empty space within the watercolor of the Christian year. It is a time for us to *celebrate* our faith, freely. It is not necessarily a time to celebrate a singular dimension of the Christian narrative, but the overall and grand dimensions of the Gospel and its message. This message is no less grand in its particular respects, but it is all the more so when observed in its entirety. I have found this wide perspective most accessible amid the dreamy atmospheres of summertime and fall, when the filters of imagination are permitted freer rein, making possible anew that blessed sense of timelessness that was so common in our youth and early childhood. It may even be that in this state of fluid contemplation mediocre Christians can imagine something of the light described by Christian saints.

The months from Pentecost to Advent are not extraordinary in and of themselves, and yet, every year, how many utterly extraordinary things take place within this season; and how many would not have come to pass, were it not for all the curious and joyous dreams that fill our Ordinary Time?

Notes

1. Eliot, T. S. *The Complete Poems and Plays 1909-1950.* (New York: Harcourt, Brace & World, 1952), pp. 21, 23.
2. *Days of the Lord: The Liturgical Year.* Vol. 4. Trans. M. Beaumont. (Collegeville, Minnesota: The Liturgical Press, 1992), p. 3.
3. *The Complete Works of Washington Irving.* Vol. 8. Ed. Haskell Springer. (Boston: Twayne Publishers, 1978), pp. 272-273.
4. Quoted in *Liturgical Spirituality*, by Philip H. Phatteicher. (Valley Forge, Pennsylvania: Trinity Press International, 1997), p. 106.
5. From "Mason Jar," by David Steinberg. Quoted from *Anthology of Magazine Verse and Year-book of American Poetry.* Ed. Alan F. Pater (Beverly Hills, California: Monitor Book Co., 1981), p. 447.
6. Ibid., p. 152.
7. Ibid., p. 6.

Chapter 8: Aesthetics in Religious Life

The highway of religious life is scattered with distraction: leisure, work, relationships, and school--legitimate concerns. The aesthetic route to spiritual perfection holds particular diversions, and those who choose this scenic road are no less prone to turn aside. In our travels we encounter vistas dotted bright with holy intimation-- virtual greenbelts of desire.

We find ourselves enamored with the holiness in nature, and may turn aside from fellowship and prayer to amble in its light. We may be drawn to fantasies of art--the liquid imagery of cinema, the shimmer of a painting, the glossy detail of a print. Enraptured by the sweetness of reflected light, we lose perspective on its source.

But merely calling God the source is wholly insufficient. According to tradition, the need for friendship with the Lord is linked to our salvation, as being either evidence of or impetus for a spiritual conversion. In scripture and in the annals of the Church this fact is stated plainly. This relationship may even wax aesthetic. This manifests most clearly for this writer in the language of romantic love.

Language of romantic love illuminates our scripture and theology. Arising in a rubric glow from off the text of "Songs," of Ruth, and of the writings of the prophets and apostles, it colors and renews our faith perspective, infusing the religious life with passion and intensity. Perhaps the synthesis of passionate devotion and aesthetics finds most elegant expression in the work of three medieval mystics: Mechthild of Magdeburg, Hadewijch of Brabant, and John (called Yepes) of the Cross.

Mechthild

Flourishing from about 1220 to about 1318, Beguines were mostly well placed European women who rejected the identity of ornamental hostess, wife, and mother, to pursue an independent spiritual vocation. Beguines included also women of less elevated class that had support by other means, or that who were willing to contribute in some other useful ways. These women formed communities, called "beguinages."

Beguines survived by offering the people of surrounding towns the services of, among other things, nursing, spinning, weaving, and embroidering. These communities were somewhat like religious orders, although without a structured rule. This appeared to be the main complaint of Church authorities, who viewed these new communities as fertile ground for heresy.

The writings of Beguines were often seen by Church authorities as evidence of this, as Beguine expression utilized romantic language difficult to gauge. In time, Beguines were forced by Church authorities to join established orders. Colorful theologies and spiritual approaches of Beguines, synthesizing literary, scriptural, and spiritual experience, remain in our tradition to this day.

Mechthild of Magdeburg embodies this tradition. Born in 1208, likely to nobility, Mechthild is, in her own words, "greeted by the Holy Spirit" (her expression for a special inundation of God's love) at the age of twelve. In her early twenties, Mechthild travels to the nearby town of Magdeburg, to live as a Beguine. Living a Beguine appears to catalyze her spiritual development. This growth is recognized by others, and later, in her forties, her confessor, the Dominican Heinrich of Halle, instructs Mechthild to write a book about her time with God. The result is Mechthild's classic work *The Flowing Light of the Godhead*.

Mechthild's writing in this work describes her love for Christ in earthy mood and metaphor. It brings to mind the "Song of Songs" and, perhaps more readily, the courtly love poems common to her day. Unlike the "Song of Songs," this genre is replete with imagery atilt toward feminine perspective, even in the writing done by males. The place of Mechthild's work within the genre of this age is seen within her many ardent calls to Christ:

> I seek you with my thoughts
> As a maiden secretly does her lover.
> I shall fall terribly sick from this,
> For I am bound to you.
> The bond is stronger than I am,
> Thus I cannot become free of love.
> I cry out to you in great longing,
> A lonely voice;
> I hope for your coming with heavy heart,
> I cannot rest, I am on fire,
> Unquenchable in your burning love.[1]

Mechthild's verse reveals also a reciprocity of love. God replies to Mechthild--and in a language as romantic as her own. Echoing the "Song of Songs," the voice of God declares: "You are like a new bride... And I shall be waiting for you in the orchard of love/And shall pluck for you the flowers of sweet union/And shall make a bed for you out of the soft grass of holy knowledge,/And the bright sun of my eternal Godhead/Shall make you radiant with the secret wonder of my attractiveness."[2]

And yet, the Lord's response to Mechthild's love is mercifully restrained: "No matter how softly I caress you,/I inflict immense pain on your poor body./If I were to surrender myself to you continuously, as you desire,/I would lose my delightful dwelling place on earth within you."[3] But Mechthild's love for God is blind to human reason. In romantic desperation she declares: "I would willingly die of love/ If it could happen to me./Him whom I love I have seen/With my beaming eyes/Present in my soul."[4]

Hadewijch

The life of Hadewijch of Brabant is less well known. There were in fact a number of devout religious women with that name between the twelfth and thirteenth centuries, and so her family remains unknown. But it is likely that, as with most Beguines, Hadewijch was of nobility, as she speaks with fluid ease of chivalry and courtly love, subjects most familiar to the upper classes. As well, her writing shows some fluency in French and Latin, and she demonstrates some competence in rhetoric, numerology, music theory, and astronomy.[5]

It is commonly believed that Hadewijch became a leader in Beguine community, but that she also made some enemies. Apparently, she had a following of younger women, eager to attain her mystical experience, but that who could not seem to do so with sufficiency--to themselves or her. Hadewijch's enemies extended also to the outside world, to laity and clergy who perceived her piety as less than totally sincere. It is postulated by historians that she was charged with heresy-- possibly of "quietism"-- and discharged from her beguinage.[6]

This would not at all have been surprising, since her work reflects a raging and affective independence. Most prominent among her theses is the passionate assertion that the Christian must "live love." It is understandable why those outside her inner circle might have been suspicious, might have seen her as a dangerous, if not a hopelessly romantic threat to Church authority.

And yet, one cannot help but sense her longing for a fellowship with God, for herself and others, expressed in fluid prose:

> O beloved, why has not Love sufficiently overwhelmed you and engulfed you in her abyss? Alas! when Love is so sweet why do you not fall deep into her? And why do you not touch God deeply enough in the abyss of his Nature, which is so unfathomable? Sweet love, give yourself for Love's sake fully to God in love.[7]

John

Yepes is another (albeit more familiar) mystic in the Church who synthesized aesthetic feel with love of Christ. His poem "The Spiritual Canticle," composed in prison, reflects this synthesis. Expanding on the "Song of Songs," it flows with verdant imagery. Working on this poem promoted John's rapport with God, but also gave to John a sense of space within his darkened cell, and so, of freedom--which doubtless helped to keep him sane. These excerpts from the canticle reveal his secret world:

> O woods and thickets
> Planted by the hand of my beloved!
> O green meadow,
> Coated, bright with flowers.
> Tell me, has he passed by you?
>
> O spring like crystal!
> If only, on your silvered-over face,
> You would suddenly form
> The eyes I have desired,
> Which I bear sketched deep within my heart.[8]

This synthesis is also found in John's short poem "The Dark Night of the Soul." Densely atmospheric, rich with metaphor, it seems a view to John's escape from prison. But of all the stanzas in the poem, the fourth remains unique. One translation reads: "Oh night thou was my guide/of night more loving than the rising sun/Oh night that joined the lover to the beloved one/transforming each of them into the other."[9] This translation is exquisite, yet extreme, as it suggests reversal of the human-God relationship--a virtual interchange of natures.

A safer view is as exquisite. It is that John describes an interchange of affect, or more accurately, of effect--a willingness by God to *share* what you are doing to his heart by having you *experience* exactly what he feels--while God, in turn, *knows* the rapture of your heart, caused by him.[10] But such a model is abstraction, described in two dimensions. The closest we may come to drafting any diagram or blueprint is analogy. Perhaps this analogue exists within romantic love, in the moment of a kiss, when lovers *sense* the rapture of each other's hearts.

Another version of this stanza reads: "O night! O guide!/O night more loving than the dawn!/O night that joined/Lover with beloved,/ Beloved in the lover transformed!"[11] Even this translation makes us pause, as it hints that Christ himself becomes transformed in some way by the union. In fairness, it may be that John's "Beloved [Christ] in the lover transformed!" speaks simply to the presence of our Lord within the convert's heart. There are more translations of this line, and each reveals a different spin. I find reciprocally experienced affect the loveliest!

Other Voices

Expressions of a love for God, endeavored through the language of aesthetics, are not restricted to distinguished writers, nor to any single age. This next account reflects that truth. Written by a woman living ages after John, its tone is intimate--and shows a core of talent. It also intimates some reciprocity of affect through the imagery of light:

Last night was the sweetest night I ever had in my life. I never before, for so long a time together, enjoyed so much of the light and rest and sweetness of heaven in my soul, but without the least agitation of body during the whole time. Part of the night I lay awake, sometimes asleep, and sometimes between sleeping and waking. But all night I continued in a constant, clear, and lively sense of the heavenly sweetness of Christ's excellent love, of his nearness to me, and of my dearness to him; with an inexpressibly sweet calmness of soul in an entire rest in him. I seemed to myself to perceive a glow of divine love come down from the heart of Christ in heaven into my heart in a constant stream, like a stream or pencil of sweet light. At the same time my heart and soul all flowed out in love to Christ, so that there seemed to be a constant flowing and reflowing of heavenly love, and I appeared to myself to float or swim, in these bright, sweet beams, like the motes swimming in the beams of the sun, or the streams of his light that come in at the window.[12]

Finally, for better or for worse, there is perhaps no greater inspiration for the Christian artist than denial of the senses. Such deprivation comes to us through varied means in life, such as poverty and hunger, in isolation during illness or in time of abject grief. Although we should not always seek these hurtful states, we should concede their worth. These seasons can refine aesthetic sense, and hone our fellowship with God. Then a work of holy affect may emerge, as in the excerpt shown below:

Jesus has come to take up his abode in my heart. It is not so much a habitation, an association, as a sort of fusion. Oh, new and blessed life! life which becomes each day more luminous... The wall before me, dark a few moments since, is splendid at this hour because the sun shines on it. Wherever its rays fall they light up a conflagration of glory; the smallest speck of glass sparkles; each grain of sand emits fire; even so there is a royal song of triumph in my heart because the Lord is there. My days succeed each other; yesterday a blue sky; today a clouded sun; a night filled with strange dreams; but as soon as the eyes open, and I regain consciousness, and seem to begin life again, it is always the same figure before me, always the same presence filling my heart.[13]

Conclusions

The aesthetic route to Christian life holds sparkling diversions. Such rest-stops are important. For though the thoroughfares of Christian life may take us far, rarely does the road retain the meaning of the journey. The weather changes, signposts dim, and Christians on the highway seek reminders of their goal.

Reminders of this goal abound within the backroads of imagination sanctified by grace. Teresa found them in the world of formal art. She writes: "At times it certainly seemed to me as if I were looking at a painting, but on many other occasions it appeared to be no painting but Christ Himself, such was the clarity with which He was pleased to appear to me."[14]

Clearly, the aesthetic things in life refresh. And yet, if they harm our fellowship or do not call us into prayer with Christ, they are merely dreams. But you have seen enough for now. It is time to start back up again. This process of restarting is itself a joy; as Jay Wickersham describes it: "now you slam the hood,/restart your car./ The road begins to move."[15] If we are faithful, the horizon of the kingdom beckons... takes us on our way.

Notes

1. Mechthild of Magdeburg. *The Flowing Light of the Godhead.* Trans. Frank Tobin. (New York: Paulist Press, 1998), p. 93.
2. Ibid., p. 95.
3. Ibid., p. 94.
4. Ibid., p. 69.
5. *Hadewijch: The Complete Works.* Trans. Columba Hart. (New York: Paulist Press, 1980), p. 5
6. Ibid., p. 4.
7. Ibid., p. 56.
8. *St. John of the Cross: Selected Writings.* Ed. Kieran Kavanaugh. (New York: Paulist Press, 1987), pp. 222-223.
9. McKennitt, Loreena. *The Mask and Mirror.* Compact Disc. (Burbank, California: Warner Bros. Records, 1994).
10. John alludes to this dynamic in another work, the "Romances." Of the Trinity he writes: "As the lover in the beloved/each lived in the other." See Doohan, Leonard, *The Contemporary Challenge of John of the Cross: An Introduction to His Life and Teaching.* (Washington, DC: ICS Publications, 1995), p. 28.
11. De Nicolas, Antonio. *St. John of the Cross: Alchemist of the Soul.* (New York: Paragon House, 1989), p. 103.
12. James, William. *The Varieties of Religious Experience.* (New York: Mentor, undated), p. 238.
13. Ibid., p. 349. This excerpt from pp. 280-283 of a book entitled *Il Vit: Six Meditations sur le Mystere Chretien,* by Wilfred Monod. Monod identifies the author of the account only as "an old man."
14. Cohen, J.M., and J-F. Phipps. *The Common Experience.* (Wheaton, Ill.: Quest Books, 1992), p. 99.
15. From "Two Scenes After Edward Hopper," quoted from *Anthology of Magazine Verse and Yearbook of American Poetry, 1997.* Ed. Alan F. Pater. (Palm Springs, California: Monitor Book Co., 1997), pp. 557-558.

Chapter 9: A Summer Meditation

At a time in my life when all was becoming noisy and run-of-the-mill, a friend from my past called me at work, and we talked of my nerve-wracked condition. Wishing to settle a personal debt, he offered to lend me his farm in the mountains. He said that it wasn't the typical farm, the sort that yielded a crop. Set in a valley in upstate New York, the farm was his private retreat.

But, said my friend, there were grapes on the land, growing profusely on ground-level vines; and that vision held me until I arrived. And when I arrived, it was night. I detected an outline of ridge, some trees, and the gurgling sound of a brook. Once in the house, I ate some light food, then made up my bed for the night. I rose about seven o'clock the next day and wandered outside to explore.

The front of the yard was scattered with trees--cherry, walnut, maple, and oak. These gave way to a meadow of grass that rolled like surf to the hills. The air, moist with dew and the summertime heat, echoed the hiss of cicada. It was "one of those gorgeous halcyon mornings of summer, of utter stillness and clearness,--a veritable *Sun*-day... when even the uncreated light seems to be palpable and visibly to permeate created things."[1]

I decided to look for the succulent grapes my friend had said covered the land. I gathered a bucket, a Bible, a notebook and pen, and set off into the meadow. In less than an hour I stumbled across the crumbling remains of a wall. Its stonework suggested an ancient decorum, like ruined Roman construction.

Miniature vines with miniature grapes had crested the top of the wall. After an hour of gathering these, I leaned on a block that was covered with moss and faded to slumbering thought. In the depths of my indolent haze, Proverbs 24: 30-34 came suddenly into my mind:

> I went past the field of the sluggard,
> past the vineyard of the man who
> lacks judgment;
> thorns had come up everywhere,
> the ground was covered with weeds,
> and the stone wall was in ruins...
> A little sleep, a little slumber,
> a little folding of the hands to rest...[1] (NIV).

Often fatigue is nothing at all but a stubborn refusal to work. I wondered awhile if I or my friend had been guilty of such misbehavior. Ecclesiastes had counseled that joy can be found in loving the work that you do. This seemed like the counsel of wisdom to me, though hardly exciting or sweet. But Wisdom herself had lamented the fact that people rejected her wares. This "farm" was a glaring reminder of discipline's muted appeal: the fields were an ocean of grass, and the farmhouse needed repair. The crumbling wall that I leaned up against accused me of sloth to my back!

The Test of Morpheus

I had always believed that work is an engine able to generate joy, so long as you had the freedom to think and what you were doing felt new. Neither of these had been so in my job; I had labored with no satisfaction. Ecclesiastes had spoken for me: "What does a man get for all the toil and anxious striving with which he labors under the sun? All his days his work is pain and grief; even at night his mind does not rest." (Ecc. 2:22-23)

Sleep has always affected my life and colored my journey with God. One product of this has been what I call the "Test of Morpheus."[2] The roots of this test lie embedded throughout Ecclesiastes, Proverbs, and Psalms. Its premise is simply that thoughts and behaviors, specifically those directed towards God and oneself, determine how well we can sleep. Proverbs 3: 21-24 is a signal example of this:

> My son, preserve sound judgment and discernment,
> do not let them out of your sight;
> they will be life for you,
> an ornament to grace your neck.
> Then you will go on your way in safety,
> and your foot will not stumble;
> when you lie down, you will not be afraid;
> when you lie down, your sleep will be sweet. (NIV)

Living in sloth is clearly rejection of wisdom's appeal for discernment. It can lead to personal ruin. But people can follow too rigid a path and end in a similar way. For instance, if I manage my life in micro detail, often my world will implode. A humorous picture of this can be seen in the film *Let It Ride*. When a cabbie (Richard Dreyfuss) has a marvelous day at the track, he budgets his winnings with paper and pen: he "pays off" all of his bills, lists the things he will buy--only to whimper "I'm broke!" before he's collected a dime. Such thinking is rarely a static event. In time it can permeate sleep.

But sometimes I sense that God wants me to act, and even to plan for the future. Often he jostles me out of my sleep and renders me restless for days. Only when I become willing to move is wholeness restored to my sleep. In lieu of a detailed plan of attack, I concentrate more on direction, on trajectory rather than steps. I choose a direction that *seems* to make sense (though nothing extreme or destructive), then leave it with God for a season. If my sleep is restored, I can only conclude the decision has weathered the Test.

If it is not, I can only conclude that the choice was not of the Lord, and then I continue to choose, *until* I recover my sleep. If none of my choices can generate sleep, the answer grows starkly apparent: the hour has come to rest from my thoughts and from any ambitious behaviors. Breathing a sigh of relief in the sun, I settled back down to a doze. Last night I had wandered the meadows of Nod.[3] My critical choice to come to the farm had weathered the Test of Morpheus.

Mending Wall

But although I had come to a happy conclusion, I felt the desire to work. I had no experience plowing a field or shingling over a house, but fixing a wall appeared simple to me. I surveyed the structure to all of its length and noted a section in need of repair. It was fallen and riddled with gaps, appearing as old and punctured a wall as the structure depicted by Frost: "Something there is that doesn't love a wall,/That sends the frozen ground-swell under it,/And spills the upper boulders in the sun,/And makes gaps even two can pass abreast."[4]

I imagined that I had been charged with the task to rebuild Jerusalem's wall. This made my adventure more pleasant and real. No Sanballat stood by to stumble my efforts; still, I pretended he did (I carried the sharpened branch of an oak, pretending that it was my spear). Holding this weapon while lifting those stones was not an easy endeavor--and it probably hindered my work. This was behavior that summed up my life. All of my life I have overprepared, in leisure and in my vocations. In Ecc.11:3-4 we read:

> If clouds are full of water,
>   they pour rain upon the earth.
> Whether a tree falls to the south or to
>   the north,
>   in the place where it falls, there will
>   it lie.
> Whoever watches the wind will not
>   plant;
> whoever looks at the clouds will not
>   reap (NIV).

While Ecclesiastes saw the need for normal preparation, he also saw that life could not be lived in fear of storms or trees blown over by the wind. I have always borrowed trouble in that way, planning for problems that didn't ensue--while life passed by around me. Considering this in greater detail, I decided to lay down my spear. Soon I'd restored my slice of the wall to something resembling its strength. Then I settled myself down to lunch. No Hittites would plunder this part of the farm. I feasted on grapes and exulted: "The precious fruit of Ephraim!"

Afternoon Reflections

Done with grapes and work for then, I ambled off to the west, over the open field. From the zenith of the cloudless sky, the sun bombarded earth with light, and all of the land before me quivered in the heat. The vision before me was like a mirage: I could almost perceive vast cascades of rays descending onto the earth. The world, in fact, appeared awash in solar radiation.

This light appeared more refined to me than sunlight in the city. But still I needed shade. The world was brilliant now, but growing hot and muggy--"Ecclesiastes weather," as I called it. And so I walked and found some maple trees beyond that band of meadow, their upper branches tangling into canopies of green. These awnings filtered sunlight in its myriad degrees, some admitting shafts, while other spots were layered almost dim. I opened up my Bible to Ecclesiastes 8:16-17, and read these words:

When I applied my mind to know wisdom and to observe man's labor on earth--his eyes not sleeping day or night--then I saw all that God has done. No one can comprehend what goes on under the sun. Despite all his efforts to search it out, man cannot discover its meaning. Even if a wise man claims he knows, he cannot really comprehend it (NIV).

This passage had meaning for me in that space. Seeking to fathom the order of God had siphoned some much needed sleep. But it had not been that goal itself that caused my sleeplessness. I had made the gross mistake of searching in *detail*, instead of using simple test and open-ended trial. Once this evil wore me out, I still could find no rest. I pounded on at work till it became a sickness. Putting off the last resort, that of seeking retreat, was fine. But I had waited far too long.

In retrospect, my error was a blessing, much as any error is. Often we may view our ignorance as sin. But what is sin but disobedience to God, who wishes us the best? And disobedience can come in more than active variations. If, for instance, God insists that we depart our nest, and we refuse, how different are we from a child who never leaves the house? Consider the story of Jonah.

Certain things you know within the confines of your mind, from textbooks and from thought. But only when you put aside the manuals and talk, and get behind the wheel, can you *taste* the open road. And sometimes after accidents you can taste it best. This principle is hinted at by Julian of Norwich, in her work entitled *Showings*. The intimation takes place in a parable in which a monarch sends his servant on a job. The servant, all too anxious to succeed, trips and falls into a ditch, where he suffers much. In language reminiscent of my quest for sleep, the author says the servant "groans and moans... tosses about and writhes."[5]

The king does not condemn the man, but praises his behavior as the consequence of zeal, worthy of reward: "See my beloved servant, what harm and injuries he has had and accepted in my service for my love, yes, and for his good will. Is it not reasonable that I should reward him for his fright and his fear, his hurt and his injuries and all his woe?"[6] Julian comments further:

> And in this an inward spiritual revelation of the lord's meaning descended into my soul, in which I saw that this must necessarily be the case, that his great goodness and his own honour require that his beloved servant, whom he loved so much, should be highly and blessedly rewarded forever, above what he would have been if he had not fallen, yes, and so much that his falling and all the woe that he received from it will be turned into high, surpassing honour and endless bliss.[7]

In the end the Lord declares to Julian that "Sin is necessary, but all will be well, and all will be well, and every kind of thing will be well."[8]

The Cool of the Day

The lowering disc of the sun was dissolving onto the ridge, and here in the deepening shade, the cool of the day had begun. The valley exuded the sweetness of summertime air, a mellowing fragrance of lilac, jasmine, and earth, but minus the sense of oppression that comes with the stifling heat. These are the happiest hours I know in a day. The lowering sun appears to remove my worries along with the heat. My work is completed and fears seem to fade like detail into the dusk.

This tendency mirrors a synchronous model of worlds--inner, external, of spirit, of mind, and of flesh. That my view of the world can be colored by light is an ample reminder of this; that my body relaxes while I am in prayer confirms that thesis for me. This truth is apparent on infinite levels, filtering through our perception. In wintertime earth can seem frozen and bleak--or lustrous, clean, and alive, depending on how we are feeling inside. In summer the world can be arid and hot, "Ecclesiastes weather," or radiant, verdant, and sweet.

My shelter of trees had provided me space, but now that the daylight was fading, I picked up my bucket, my Bible, my notebook and pen, and wandered back into the field. Crickets were starting to sing, and Venus had pierced the horizon. High constellations began to emerge: Lyra the harp, Cygnus the swan (known as the Northern Cross), Hercules, Lynx, and Lacerta. I lumbered away in the general direction the farmhouse seemed to have lain. And when I got back it was dark.

The Focus of Night

Approaching the porch of the house, I looked to the sky and gave thanks. The luminous dust of creation proclaimed the resplendence of God: the heavens enormous, littered with light--haunted with faint nebulae, and stardust too dense to be reckoned. Beneath this tremendous diffusion of light I staggered in awestruck communion. Pouring my consciousness out to the Lord, I was filled with a consummate love, expressed in a holy negation. The following excerpt, taken from James, intimates what I recall:

> I remember the night, and almost the very spot on the hilltop, where my soul opened out, as it were, into the Infinite, and there was a rushing together of the two worlds, the inner and the outer. It was deep calling unto deep -- the deep that my own struggle had opened up within being answered by the unfathomable deep without; reaching beyond the stars. I stood alone with Him who had made me, and all the beauty of the world. I did not seek Him, but felt the perfect unison of my spirit with His. It was like the effect of some great orchestra when all the separate notes have melted into one swelling harmony that leaves the listener conscious of nothing save that his soul is being wafted upwards, and almost bursting with its own emotion. The perfect stillness of the night was thrilled by a more solemn silence. The darkness held a presence that was all the more felt because it was not seen.[9]

Before me the farmland lay silent and black, save for the song of the wakening cricket and the light of the fireflies' spark. I sensed an expansion inside of my heart that opened it wide as the sky. My day out of doors had altered my view of all I had come here to find. I reckoned that I had been lost in a dream, and only just now had awakened. I could see that, through all of my pious reflections on faith, thinking had governed my sight. I could number the reasons against its employment, yet only by using my brain--and that vision had seemed so transcendent!

What I discovered that ravishing night I had secretly known in my heart, and yet, it had lingered elusive. But I sensed that it isn't important to know in the confines of temporal time. Someday, I promised myself, I will realize the secrets of heaven and earth--when God gives me transcendent perspective. For now, in this world, I need only to trust in God's competent hand, and to listen with all of my heart, the avenue of his refreshment.

Notes

1. Wilmshurst, W.L. *Contemplations: Being Studies in Christian Mysticism.* (Kila, Montana: Kessinger, 1994), p. 144.
2. "The Arms of Morpheus" has long been used as a poetic name for sleep.
3. "The Land of Nod" is sometimes used as a poetic name for sleep.
4. Frost, Robert. *Early Poems by Robert Frost.* (New York: Crown Publishers, 1981), p. 80.
5. Julian of Norwich. *Showings.* (Mahwah, New Jersey: Paulist, 1978), p. 267.
6. Ibid., p. 268.
7. Ibid., p. 269.
8. Ibid., p. 225.
9. James, William. *The Varieties of Religious Experience.* (New York: Mentor, undated), p. 73.

Chapter 10: The Dark Night of the Soul

The Dark Night of the Soul has always been a part of our tradition. Although coined by John of the Cross, the term has doubtless gone by other names. In scripture and the annals of the Church, it is depicted as a season of uncertainty--sometimes fraught with pain-- that facilitates transition. Christ himself endured this night while in Gethsemane, and for three dramatic hours on the cross. Paul faced it in his blindness. It *is* the book of Job. The Dark Night holds no less relevance for us, although in altered form. Filtered through the prism of contemporary life, it holds the meaning given it by John--but with an emphasis for *now*.

St. John depicts the Dark Night as a season of purgation--not of fleshly but of sensory desire. God weans the Christian from pursuing him through intellect and sense, by dampening the function of those routes. In time, these routes wax obsolete and cease to work at all. Ultimately, the approach of mind is jettisoned, allowing God a greater ease of access to our *hearts*: "The soul detaches itself from sense... basing itself on faith, that it may afterwards travel along the strait road of the other night of the spirit, by which it advances toward God in most pure faith, which is the means of union with Him."[1]

John notes that people often fail to recognize the hand of God in this ordeal. So used to being in control, the human mind is loath to abdicate its role, even for its good. To illustrate, John compares this to "a child kicking and crying in order to walk when his mother wants to carry him" or to a person moving a painting "back and forth while the artist is at work on it."[2]

A second, more contemporary view is nowhere as dogmatic. It depicts the Dark Night as confusing, but without the sense of abject pain contained in John's description.[3] Gerald May writes that "To be fully accurate, one should probably not call the dark night an 'experience' at all. It is more a deep and ongoing process of unknowing that involves the loss of habitual experience."[4]

As with John's, this paradigm describes transition to a higher stage of growth; and as with John's, progress to transition can be stifled both by active efforts to resist--or to *hasten* the transition. Echoing the saint, Gerald May insists: "If one tries very hard to 'produce' spiritual experiences during a period of emptiness, the result will almost certainly be frustration. If this approach is not radically shifted or if one does not permit oneself to give up at this time, the frustration may well become destructive."[5]

Another model of the Dark Night of the Soul is markedly more practical, as it involves disruption of external aspects in our life. This may take the form of unemployment, illness, loss of a loved one, natural disaster, and so forth. Focus on such practical dimensions opens up the subject to psychologists, like Elizabeth Kubler-Ross and others.

As with the other models, the impulse to control is strong, and it is rare for people in this state to instantly relinquish all control to God. It is only when our thinking yields that we can transcend our confusion. And, as in the other models that I've mentioned in this chapter, the goal is perseverance, and ultimately, emergence from the process, stronger, and with renewed perspective. The examples of Job, and particularly of Kubler-Ross, are germane here.

Kubler-Ross believed that people pass through certain stages while in grief: denial, anger, bargaining, depression, and acceptance. While Kubler-Ross was not a Christian (at least as I define it), her model is intrinsic to the field of spiritual direction, as each stage intimates relationship with God (e.g.: bargaining and anger). And, as in the other models that I've mentioned, one emerges (ideally) with perspective that is able to accommodate the change.

And yet, despite the implication of consistent sequence in these models, the option of exception is allowed. Teresa of Avila, who, along with John, represents the more dogmatic of the models, writes:

"There is no state of prayer so exalted that it will not be necessary to return to the beginnings."[6] John himself reminds us that "God leads each one along different paths." He urges us not to "tyrannize souls and deprive them of their freedom..." and to "judge for yourself the breadth of the evangelical doctrine."[7]

May writes that "God-given experiences such as glimpses of the dark night are never really reducible to such specifics. There are always exceptions and surprises..." and "whenever spiritual directors use any kind of criteria for objective evaluation as a substitute for their own prayerful, surrendered openness of heart, they do an injustice to their directees."[8] Finally, nowhere in her work does Kubler-Ross insist the stages in her model are embedded, sequentially, in stone.

Connecting all the models is a sense of limitation--of our ideas, abilities, creativity, and spiritual perspective. This begs the issue of surrender, of *everything* we are, to God, including, among other things, our imagination: not for its destruction, but that it might be sanctified and thus be used by God. John concedes that this may even yield the vision sought by sensate means: "In this way the soul draws nearer and nearer to the divine union, in darkness, by the way of faith which, though it be also obscure, yet sends forth a marvelous light."[9]

Ultimately, the Dark Night is a challenge to expand our faith by our relinquishing control to God. Walter Kasper writes:

> What is faith here other than a total self-abandonment to God's promise and call, a letting go of all human security, a holding to and standing fast in God's world alone. Faith here is a fundamental decision, which results from a conversion from one's normal attitude and one's normal security, a standing fast independent of all human security, a trust and a confidence in God alone.[10]

This challenge can evoke discomfort in the Church, most profoundly in believers needing crisis-oriented spiritual direction, many of whom, ironically, are blind to stress they cause themselves through worry. Spiritual directors might respond by offering the metaphor of Sabbath[11]--the Dark Night as a rest from our defenses.

71

Described this way, the Dark Night of the Soul resembles other, less expansive seasons in our spiritual experience, encountered in the past. By so demystifying this ordeal, approaches to those tests might then emerge to present application--and to the greater process of the Christian life.

Notes

1. *The Dark Night of the Soul.* Trans. Benedict Zimmerman. (Cambridge: James Clarke & Co. Ltd., 1973), p. 52. Hereafter referred to as *Dark Night.*
2. Green, Thomas H. "The First Blind Guide: John of the Cross and Spiritual Direction." (*Spiritual Life*, Summer 1991), pp. 72-73. Hereafter referred to as "Blind Guide."
3. *Dark Night*, p. 34.
4. May, Gerald G. *Care of Mind/Care of Spirit: A Psychiatrist Explores Spiritual Direction.* (San Francisco: Harper San Francisco, 1992), p. 107. Hereafter referred to as *Care of Mind.*
5. Ibid., p. 103.
6. Leech, Kenneth. *Soul Friend: The Practice of Christian Spirituality.* Intro. Henri Nouwen. (San Francisco: Harper & Row Publishers, 1977), p. 151.
7. "Blind Guide," pp. 75-76.
8. *Care of Mind*, pp. 110-111.
9. Lewis, David. *The Complete Works of St. John of the Cross.* Vol. 1. (London: Longman, Roberts, and Green, 1864), p. 64. Also, *Life of St. John of the Cross*, by David Lewis. (London: Thomas Baker, 1897), pp. 108-109, contains a description of John's encounter with the heavenly light while in prison: "One night the friar who kept him went as usual to see that his prisoner was safe, and witnessed the heavenly light with which the cell was flooded. He did not stop to consider it, but hurried to the prior, thinking that someone in the house had keys to open the doors of the prison. The prior, with two religious went at once to the prison, but on his entering the room through which the prison was approached, the light vanished. The prior, however, entered the cell, and, finding it dark, opened the lantern with which he had provided himself, and asked the prisoner who had given him light. St. John answered him, and said that no one in the house had done so, that no one could do it, and that there was

neither candle nor lamp in the cell... St. John, at a later time, told one of his brethren that the heavenly light, which God so mercifully sent him, lasted the night through, and that it filled his soul with joy and made the night pass away as if it were but a moment."
10. Kasper, Walter. *Transcending All Understanding.* (San Francisco: Ignatius Press, 1989), p. 52.
11. Squire, Aelred. *Asking the Fathers: The Art of Meditation and Prayer.* (Wilton, Conn.: Morehouse-Barlow Co. and New York: Paulist Press, 1973), pp. 206-207.

Chapter 11: The Imagination in Retreat

Like detail in a painting's negative dimensions, the background of a Christian's spiritual retreat can hold the key to the effect of that retreat. Indeed, our willingness to recognize this can determine our success in weathering the season of the Dark Night. The key therein lies in the process of our spiritual perception--the challenge of "discernment." Often the solution to the challenge of discernment lies in distancing ourselves from specified objectives, embedded in the foreground of our view. This principle evokes the very rationale for spiritual retreat: withdrawal--from ineffective and exhausting patterns of devotion and behavior, patterns that *erode* our spiritual imagination.

This erosion takes its toll on spiritual advancement over time. Moreover, after such erosion has ensued, the option of withdrawal often fades from view, or, if it does remain at all, appears to us the avenue of sloth and irresponsibility. Fatigue is even taken as the evidence of faith, and as comfort that our character is sound. Such erosion argues for the "negative" approach: the abandonment of seeking God through mental concentration.

Paradoxically, departure from this altered world of spiritual perception will necessitate that we adjust our focus to exclude the very thing we seek; only then is hidden insight likely to emerge into the fore of our imagination. Only when we use "averted" vision do the background and the foreground of our field of view reverse. A similar dynamic is apparent in the skills of day and nighttime driving, and in the field of optics overall.

In daylight driving, objects are most accurately perceived directly, with "convergent" vision, while nighttime driving calls for indirect, "divergent" gaze. Likewise, in looking through a telescope at night, brighter objects such as planets or the moon are best observed directly, while fainter objects such as nebulae and galaxies are best observed by looking from the corner of one's eye.

One recalls the Asian proverb (here paraphrased from memory): "The blind are best equipped to fathom the obscure," and poet Theodore Roethke's famous line: "In a dark time, the eye begins to see.[1]" Hence, the negative approach to spiritual discernment can be the strategy of choice for Christians going through the season of the Dark Night of the Soul. This dynamic underlies the "sanctified imagination," the paradox of negative ascetical devotions turning out imaginations equal or superior in quality to those produced by direct concentration.

Clearly, direct concentration has its place in seasons of empowerment. Such imagination has been sanctified directly from our Lord and needs no purging in the void of dark experience. Both Teresa and St. John (called Yepes) of the Cross were subject to the negative perspective so prevalent in late-medieval European culture. Yet both continued to accept imagination as a means of reaching and describing God. Teresa even cultivated direct concentration, developing her visual perception by creatively observing objects found in nature, such as "a field, or water, or flowers"--noting that they drew her thoughts to God.[2]

Moreover, both Teresa and St. John describe repeated visions-- "consolations"--through wonderfully creative language, as this description of God's glory by Teresa illustrates:

It is not a radiance which dazzles, but a soft whiteness and an infused radiance which, without wearying the eyes, causes them the greatest delight... So different from any earthly light is the brightness and light now revealed to the eyes that, by comparison with it, the brightness of our sun seems quite dim and we should never want to open our eyes again for the purpose of seeing it. It is as if we were to look at a very clear stream, in a bed of crystal, reflecting the sun's rays.[3]

This focus on imagination can be a relatively minor part of Catholic life for some believers, periodic rests in seasons laboring for God. And so, we do ourselves a favor by remembering the lives of Christian saints who offered some perspective not only on the foreground of our spiritual experience, but on the value of its "negative" dimensions, and who considered the necessity of sharing with the greater Church accounts of their refreshment, consolations, foretastes of our heavenly reward.

Notes

1. Roethke, Theodore. *The Far Field: The Last Poems of a Major American Poet.* (Garden City, New York: Doubleday & Company, Inc., 1964), p. 79.
2. Teresa of Avila. *The Life of Teresa of Jesus: The Autobiography of St. Teresa of Avila.* Trans. E. Allison Peers. Ed. E. Allison Peers. Intro. E. Allison Peers. (Garden City, New York: Image Books, 1960), p. 18.
3. Ibid., pp. 260-261.

Chapter 12: An Autumn Meditation

For the Nuns at Mt. St. Michael's, Spokane, Washington

Some of the holiest hours I've known have been in autumnal weather. Many of these occurred in my youth, in the suburbs of central Long Island. This was a part of the state of New York that could not be labeled as city. Neither, however, could it be grouped with the rural-based townships that lay on the east of the island. Our parish was balanced between these two worlds, yet it sported a rustic mystique.

Clapboard colonial houses reflected a linear symmetry, much like the pattern of housing encountered in Brooklyn or downtown Manhattan--but, set on an acre of wooded terrain, each was a space to itself. Here, in the landscapes of gilded October, closeness to God might often ensue with only a walk to the park. Such was the case when I was sixteen, and thinking a lot about life.

By middle October the heat had abated and foliage colored our parish. This world was a series of neighborhoods lit with the delicate rusting of scarlet, burnt orange, and maize, a motionless riot of color that buried our driveways and lawns. The path that I followed away from my house was covered in dew-frosted leaves. This was a path I had followed in peace for most of my childhood years. This day it would lead me to somewhere beyond.

The damp morning air was filling with sun and the buzz of a neighborhood saw. In the branches above me a crow gave its call, and a woodpecker tapped in the distance. The school, like a fortress of windows and brick, lay off to the right of the path; I bore to the left, and steadied my eyes on the tangle of trees up ahead. This was the park that I so often came to when nothing remained of my world, when parents and friends seemed as distant to me as the thought of my fortieth year.

Approaching the entrance of sentinal oaks, the tangle of branches unwove. Distant perspective had made these seem dense and gnarled into something grotesque. Now they were open to all of the sky, a robin's egg blue or cerulean tint that flooded the ground with its light. This entrance of trees has always appealed to my sense of adventure in God. In autumn it held a particular thrill, as if I were seeing it for the first time.

A sylvan geometry styled this world--a beauty of function and form, like brilliant landscape architecture sparkling in the sunlight: the groundwork inside the entrance was textured with water and glistening leaves; rivulets trickled from out of a hill and spread on the forest floor in intricate patterns that wove in between the trunks of its separate trees. Each rivulet carried a surface of leaves that wended its way through the park.

This was a day for passionate prayer, a season of desperate thoughts. My home life had turned to a drama of pain, and I needed retreat to what I considered the holiest spot in my world. This park was a sacred location to me for reasons that nobody knows. Here in the wilderness part of our town I healed from these personal wounds. This park was my Elim, my "land of the seventy palms."[1]

My prayer on this outlying fringe of the park consisted of mostly requests. I asked of the Lord the reasons for why my world had been turned on its ear. There wasn't an answer (that I could perceive), only the whisper of breeze. I couldn't discern if this was God's voice or only a zephyr of fall. I knew that Elijah had listened for God and heard him in only a whisper. I wondered if God had replied to my prayers in an equally delicate voice.

Why did I wish to know all the causes behind the effects in my life? I don't see a rational reason for this--anymore--pursuing the details of God, looking to find the mechanics of life or hoping to fathom the future. I've long since concluded that having that view would hurtle one's life into chaos. The prospect of knowing these infinite things should terrify rational people. Having that view would make us afraid to climb out of bed in the morning. This is ironic if what we've desired is greater control in our lives.

Autumn Burnings

The mid-morning air was bracing and damp, but delicious to breathe. I had always been driven to think in this air; it fired my youthful ambition. This atmosphere seemed to remove any limits from normally tame speculation. Often convinced that I'd stumbled across the contents of God's own cognition, I would float through my day in a rapturous state, wondering where to go next. This usually lasted until I arrived at the critical threshold of proof.

Wafting obscurely into this air, the pungence of leafsmoke descended. Somewhere beyond my limited view a neighbor was tending a fire. The image of smoldering leaves by the road embodies the autumn for me. In "Autumn Burnings," by Peter Desy, this image is captured in full:

My mother used to smell
my clothes to see if I'd been
near a fire. Back then, when
fall's leaves were burned
on streets, I'd stand close to watch
the season's leavings smoldering,
the deep orange core glowing.
I like to close my eyes,
knowing there was wisdom
in that burning, some gorgeous finality
I could feel, standing there. I hugged
that smoke blowing through my clothes,
a new wind biting my cheeks;
stood solitary watch, the beautiful
consummations all along the street.[2]

But somehow I managed to find in that smoke reminders of personal pain. My home life was slowly combusting it seemed, and Jesus was nowhere in sight. The problem of evil obstructed my thoughts, my prayers, and even my faith in the Lord. Soon, I began to complain. My thinking was nothing original; theodicy rarely is new. The models for why Christians suffer revolve around three or four primary themes.

One is that God is a hater of sin, and that we are abundantly sinful, even if we are forgiven through Christ. This view does not argue that Jesus has failed to pay for the sins of the world--only that punishment still is dispensed, as discipline coming from God. I have no particular problem with this, but as a young man of only sixteen, I saw it as grossly unfair. That "the Lord disciplines those he loves, as a father the son he delights in" (Prov. 3:12 NIV) held minimal logic to me.

A second is that the problem of pain has nothing to do with our sin, anymore--that all of the suffering Christians endure has a basis in natural law. Some people argue that this was a theme showcased in Solomon's writing, centuries prior to Christ. A third explanation is, simply, that Christians are targets of hell; that malice from Satan and all the unsaved results in the anguish we feel. Jesus himself guarenteed that "In the world you will have tribulation" (John 16: 33).

A fourth reason given for why Christians hurt is obscure and detached from debate. It is found in the writings of Job and Sirach. The management style of God is depicted in these as out of our cognitive range. We are hindered from knowing his system's details, and so we are ignorant of its mechanics. This model implies that the human perspective is blinded not only to cause, but to even the ultimate role of effect. And so we are told that we ought to have faith in the management style of God. In Sirach 3: 22-24 (NRSV) we read:

> Reflect upon what you have been commanded,
> for what is hidden is not your concern.
> Do not meddle in matters that are beyond you,
> for more than you can understand has been shown you.

These were all answers I could not accept. I wanted the reasons for loneliness, poverty, sickness, and doubt. I burned with a passion that verged on an anger toward everything God had commanded. I cried at the top of my lungs to the Lord: "Why? Why does this happen to *us*?" In the midst of fighting this blasphemous rage, I fell in the presence of God, in which I heard only a cryptic reply: "This isn't the minor leagues."

Epilogue

I could not decipher what the words meant--nor could my companions in church. They told me to drop it and leave it with God, that time would determine its meaning. I have mentioned this message to no one since then, for fear that it wasn't from God, and that I'd be seen as eccentric, or worse. Wilmshurst describes an identical bind. Taking a similar route as myself, he leaves the decision to others:

> Such is the imperfect narrative of something that occurred some years ago. I have never before written it; seldom spoken of it; so few there are who understand. Publish it if you will--*ad majorem Dei gloriam*, and for the encouragement of others. But let it be without a name.[3]

The kaliedoscope mornings of Long Island autumns can give one a change of perspective. And this is what happened that day in October, some thirty-one years in the past. What I'd been groaning about by the park eventually turned for the best; the pain that I suffered so long in my family helped me to grow in the Lord. My life up till now, though less than ideal, has given me hope for the future. I've never been married, had any kids, or held down a powerful job. But God has bequeathed to me all that I need, in the promise of Jesus his son.

My life has begun to resemble a monk's. It retains a dimension of stress, but still, I have made my decision to walk with my focus on heavenly things. Matthew 6:21 speaks to the need for having this view: "For where your treasure is, there your heart will be also." This is a promise on which I have based the bulk of my temporal life.

October continues to render me drunk with its color and soft, burnished light. I find that I need to restrain my opinions when autumn infuses the land--for the sake of my public and personal face. But autumnal air, though sweet in itself, fills me with mellow nostalgia; it nudges me back to that seminal day, when, weeping in foliage of copper and gold, I fell in the presence of God.

The answer I got to the problem of pain was cryptic and muted at best. My hope is that you who have sacrificed all will weigh it and find consolation. The imagery found in this chapter of love communicates what I remember. May it ease some degree of your temporal pain, and fill you with longings of palpable sweetness... like low, orange sunlight draping a garden of maize.

Notes

1. Exodus 15: 27 (NIV) reads, "Then they [the Israelites] came to Elim, where there were twelve springs and seventy palm trees, and they camped there near the water."
2. Quoted from *Anthology of Magazine Verse and Yearbook of American Poetry, 1986-88.* Ed. Alan F. Pater. (Beverly Hills, California: Monitor Book Co., 1988), p. 128.
3. Wilmshurst, W.L. *Contemplations: Being Studies in Christian Mysticism.* (Kila, Montana: Kessinger, 1994), p. 152.

Chapter 13: The Celebration of All Saints

No solemnity or feast within the Christian calendar so perfectly reflects the total Church as does the feast of All Saints. Observed the first day of November, it bids us to remember Christians gathered to the Lord, our connection with their lives and with each other. It reminds us of our common path as Christians here on earth, and of our common share as residents of heaven. It is a celebration of the Church on both sides of eternity.

The practice of revering Christian saints was borne of persecution. The early Christian martyrs formed the core of what became the catalogue of saints. When persecution stopped, ascetics' names were added to these lists, called *martyrologies*. The earliest account of any formal feast that celebrates these saints is in the Eastern Churches (in the fifth century). In time, this feast of "All the Saints" was taken west to Rome.

In the East, this feast was held the Sunday after Pentecost. But Pope Gregory the Great (590-604) would designate that time the Ember Days of Spring, and shift the feast of "All the Saints" up to November 1st. This date remained intact until the time of Boniface IV. On May 13, 610, this pope transformed the Roman Pantheon into a shrine for Christian saints. In conjunction with this act, the pontiff moved the feast to May 13, the day of the conversion. This date stayed fixed till 835, when Pope Gregory IV restored the feast of "All Saints" to November 1st, where it stands today.

While All Saints celebrates the family of Christians overall, its most distinctive element remains the role of Christian saints before the throne of God. Their role is not at all unlike the function of the "host of heaven"--that of intercession, facilitation, and even personal participation. Precedents for this tradition arise throughout the Bible, as in I Kings 22: 19-20 (NIV): "I saw the Lord sitting on his throne with all the host of heaven standing around him on his right hand and on his left. And the Lord said, 'Who will lure Ahab into attacking Ramoth Gilead and going to his death there?' One suggested this, and another that." Clearly, scripture validates the argument that God continues to respect the freewill of believers in eternity. God is no more interested in leading spiritual somnambulists in heaven than he is on earth, and so, he continues to solicit faithful intercession and participation in his work. It is also clear that such a host is not comprised of angels only (Rev. 4: 4-11). Hence, I would argue here, if Enoch and Elijah, why not other saints of God?

But of course this does not mean we bow before these saints of God as if they were the Lord himself, though both are resurrected and in glory. For we remember that the glory of the saints is but reflected light from Christ himself. A lyrical expression of this truth preserves both sanctity and separation:

> They come in singing,
> the saved ones;
> immense fresco of joy,
> love with a thousand faces
> that form one image
> in the light,
> the only icon of glory:
> Jesus Christ! [1]

Clearly, the glory of the resurrected saints is recognized in Christian liturgy--in the context of the Body overall. One passage from the *Days of the Lord* articulates this sentiment in imagistic prose:

> The brilliance of the saints comes from the same unique source of light that fills all of them. But no one of us shines

with all the light by ourselves or keeps for ourselves that part of glory that we have received. On the contrary, we are happy to see our own light shine on the others, just as we joyfully and gratefully welcome the light we receive from them.[2]

The feast of All Saints gives the Church a *vertical* connection--a sense of continuity to Christian friends awaiting our arrival. This sense reminds us that we labor never for ourselves--but for the friends around us and *beyond*. This was recognized by Christian martyrs from the start. Their willingness to suffer rather than betray their fellow saints reveals this fact. Exemplary believers in our day should also have this willingness to serve, to sacrifice their funds, their hospitality, and if need be, their life, for those they'll meet again.

This vision of reunion in eternity should deepen our concern for family and friends who risk the staining of their crowns. The Christian of today may also guide, through spiritual direction, those who openly reject eternal life. Doing so may well entail some light degree of preaching. But this need not be the sort of talk that tears the person down--but rather, the sort that tempts her with the imagery of life and of a sweet communion with the saints.

In *Days of the Lord*, we see again a passage that reflects the sentiment of unity in light, yet keeps intact the sense of individual identity intrinsic to freewill:

> The Church invites all the voices of the world to join their voices with theirs, to sing the praise of God whose holiness shines into infinity. Just as the countless stars, no matter what their size, shine with the brilliance of the sun, all those who are irradiated by the light of holiness become in God's heaven a multitude of brilliant rays of light reflecting Christ's glory.[3]

The feast of All Saints rises like a bridge across infinity. But it is more. It is an intersection of *our* earthly life with Christians who have lived before us--and of our hopeful expectation with the saints' in heaven now. It is indeed a celebration of the Church on both sides of eternity. The Christian seeking something more need look no further than the Church, those with whom she'll spend eternal life. The desert fathers knew this secret well, and put the law of hospitality to practice in their faith. Catholics today should keep this fresh in mind. For, in the words of Rainier Maria Rilke: "Your house is the last before infinity, whoever you are." [4]

Notes

1. *Days of the Lord: The Liturgical Year.* Vol. 7. Trans. Madeleine Beaumont & Mary Misrahi. (Collegeville, Minnesota: The Liturgical Press, 1994), p. 237.

2. Ibid., p. 250.

3. Ibid., p. 250.

4. Quoted in *Take Nothing for the Journey: Meditations on Time and Place*, by Donagh O'Shea. (Dublin: Dominican Publications, 1990), 1st page (unnumbered).

Chapter 14: The Hope of All Souls

The solemnity of All Souls on November 2nd expands the feast of All Saints Day. But while All Saints highlights veneration of those resurrected Christians within a general celebration of the Church, All Souls highlights intercession for those Christians still asleep, and of death's assuredness for Christians still alive. All Souls bears this similarity to Lent, but is nonetheless distinctive. For, although both Lent and All Souls focus on the theme of death, Lent projects ahead to Easter, while the feast of All Souls underscores the Church's resurrection.

Like many early Christian ways, the practice of our praying for the dead pre-dates the Christian age. In pagan Rome this practice was continued by the first believers, although in an altered form. For while pagans offered prayers to their departed, they were offered to that person's spirit. Early Christians, believing that the dead would sleep until their resurrection, prayed simply that the slumber of the righteous would be sweet.

Early Christian tombs contained inscriptions that requested prayer for the departed. In time, those prayers appeared within the liturgy. St. Cyril, the fourth century bishop of Jerusalem, writes: "We pray also for the holy Fathers and Bishops who have fallen asleep, and generally for all who have gone before us, believing that this will be of the greatest benefit to the souls of those on whose behalf our supplication is offered in the presence of the holy, the most dread Sacrifice."[1]

Comment on these early prayers suggests a scintillating prism of liturgical perspectives. For instance, this statement by Cyril would seem to indicate a less than crystallized consensus on the deadline for redemption:

> I know that many of you say: "What does it avail a soul departing this world, whether with or without sins, to be remembered at the Sacrifice?" Well, suppose a king banished persons who had offended him, and then their relatives wove a garland and presented it to him on behalf of those undergoing punishment, would he not mitigate their sentence? In the same way, offering our supplications to Him for those who have fallen asleep, even though they be sinners, we, though we weave no garland, offer Christ slain for our sins, propitiating the merciful God on both their and our own behalf.[2]

Praying for departed souls continued through medieval times among the Church religious, though they tended to restrict this observation to departed from their local ranks. Amalarius of Metz (780-850) sought to broaden this tradition. Amalarius was active in the court of Charlemagne, and studied under Alcuin, the notable reformer. Amalarius suggested that a feast be held each year wherein *all* the Church would recognize these dead.

But it was not to be within his life. It remained for St. Odilo, abbot of the Benedictines based in Cluny, to bring this issue to the fore. Odilo (ca. 962-1049) requested such a feast be held throughout the Benedictine order. In 998, Pope Sylvester II granted his request, and, in time, the feast was spread throughout the Roman Church. The feast attained the status of a listing in the Missal on June 30, 1570.

All Souls is today a somewhat minor feast; yet it serves a purpose that no other day can fill. It serves to mollify the grief we feel for loved ones now departed. It also calms the apprehension and resistance we may feel in sensing *our* mortality. It also calms our disbelief-- which even steadfast Christians will experience at times. In *Days of the Lord* we read:

> The Bible is full of instances of this anguished doubting. But at the same time, from earliest antiquity, it has also spoken, timidly at first, and then with more

assurance, of an afterlife: a mysterious other world, another life impossible to imagine, and finally, of resurrection.[3]

This is hope for Christians living on the earth today, for those who suffer exploitation, torture, and disease, who long for rest as ancients did for Sheol. It is also hope for ordinary Christians feeling lost. But unlike saints who lived before the time of Christ, we have knowledge of a hope that compensates for all our pain and memory of sins. This is the hope of All Souls.

Notes

1. *The Works of Saint Cyril of Jerusalem.* Vol. 2. Trans. Leo P. McCauley & Anthony A. Stephenson. (Washington, D.C.: The Catholic University of America Press, 1970), p. 197.
2. Ibid., p. 198.
3. Ibid., p. 277.

Chapter 15: A Memory of All Souls

Composed November 2nd 2002, Spokane, Washington

I

In the dim, dissolving sunlight of November afternoons, these skeletal horizons--static tangles of denuded trees impinging on the tungsten gray of autumn sky, speak to me of life and of redemption. Amid such atmospheres I contemplate dark memories of youth that offer consolation and rebuttal to my sometimes melancholy visions and reflections, and often to the news of imminent disaster. Such imagery in nature can inoculate one's soul against the trauma of reality--even trauma brought about by sudden, unexpected gain. That this imagery is paired for me with memories of actual misfortune concentrates such stark November days, focuses my vision to accommodate the future.

Such memories remain with me of one November day, in nineteen ninety-eight, when I had only recently been fired from my job, and could not pay my rent. I had spent that day in endless searching for employment, with minimal success. My spirit and my body were depleted, and I felt done with life. Instead of walking up the endless flight of stairs to my apartment door, where likely my attentive landlord would be waiting, I hobbled down the avenue to watch the setting sun. Beside a dead-end sign that signaled my location, an open space of trees revealed the disc, emerging briefly through the clouds.

The sun refracted through the clouds an almost hostile, lurid red, like blood; but in seconds even this began to fade. As the sun dissolved once more into the clouds, I dropped lethargic to the earth. As I was lying on the grass, the image of the sky had seemed familiar, a picture from a poem that I had loved. In better times the poem had brought to mind those elements that are, for me, the essence of the autumn: beauty and completion; but now, filtered through my melancholy vision, it evoked malaise: "Now days begin to darken at both ends/as apples do, the heavy red of sun/ at rising, setting."[1]

The image of the sun dissolving into clouds supplied appropriate reprise to my endeavors: an ending heavy and as shrouded as the sunrise had appeared to me that morning--dreary to be sure, and filled with dry routine. Ecclesiastes spoke to this routine: "The sun rises and the sun sets, and hurries back to where it rises" (Ecc. 1:5). But even consciousness of drudgery was rapidly dissolving; and losing even this sensation of existence, I halfway entertained the option of retreating to the graveyard for appropriate companions.

II

The narrow path that led into the graveyard was a gauntlet of denuded branches, skeletal and stark. Walking through this landscape, seemingly devoid of life, I wondered if the byways in the underworld were analogues to ours, or if I shared this very path with souls of the departed. Similar questions arose as I walked--and were promptly disposed of by questions that rose in their place. In time I arrived at the cusp of the graveyard, which beckoned to me like the promise of permanent slumber. The tombstones lay only a few feet away--and yet, something restrained me from going inside.

I lingered about in this shadowy world, lulled by its negative beauty--a stark, blasted landscape, stripped of all foliage, set against overcast sky. But I realized that nightfall was not far away and that dampness was slowly encroaching. I wanted to cross, but some indistinct force--God, holy angels, or maybe the dead--restrained me from leaving the path. Instead, I followed the graveyard's perimeter, and noticed, just off of its northerly edge, a shelter of sorts, garnished with colorful candles and wreaths. At first I was puzzled, and then I remembered, two things: that today was the feast of All Souls, and that this was a graveyard where service was held on that day.

As I drew near to the primitive shelter, I felt a desire to pray--or to meditate; I cannot provide details concerning this impulse, even today, for somehow my sense of direction and logic had lapsed. I was immersed in a sense of communion with God, a feeling of awe and surrender, colored with some revelation, ineffable, but somehow, essential. An experience similar to what I describe is depicted in *The Ordeal of Richard Feverel*:

> Richard was walking hurriedly. The green drenched weeds lay all about in his path, bent thick, and the forest drooped glimmeringly. Impelled as a man who feels a revelation mounting obscurely to his brain, Richard was passing one of those little forest-chapels, hung with votive wreaths, where the peasant halts to kneel and pray. Cold, still, in the twilight it stood, raindrops pattering round it. He moved by. But not many steps had he gone ere his strength went out of him, and he shuddered. What was it? He asked not. He was in other hands.[2]

III

As with any experience related to God, I cannot be sure of its source--it may simply have been the product of stress--and yet, I regard its *effects* to this day. And even today, as I struggle to sketch the event, I count those effects as a blessing. That day had been fading to darkness, but I had not entered therein. I wandered alone, back down the path, walked up the road to my place, climbed up the long flight of stairs to my room, made plans with my landlord, and peace with my God, trusting that what would await me thereafter would be for the best. Four years have passed since my brush with the dead, and life has continued as ever.

I wonder sometimes if that grisly ordeal--of which I have spared you depressing details--was something that needed to happen for me, to mirror some meaning concerning my life, or to realize some aspect in God's larger plan. That prospect imbues me with reason for hope, for faith in an all-knowing God. It renews my perspective on temporal life, on eternity, and even the Church, even now: the dim, dissolving sunlight of an All Souls afternoon diffuses the spectral image of death while beckoning to the eternal.

Notes

1. From "The Apple Sellers," by James Scruton; quoted from *Anthology of Magazine Verse and Yearbook of American Poetry, 1997*. Ed. Alan F. Pater. (Palm Springs, California: Monitor Book Co., 1997), p. 459.

2. Meredith, George. *The Ordeal of Richard Feverel.* (New York: The Modern Library, Inc., 1927), pp. 557-558.

Chapter 16: Catholic Near-Death Spirituality

The literature of near-death experience shimmers with the promise of the gospel hope. Evoking the faintest tinge of revelation or remembrance in the Christian mind, it stirs the heart. From the earliest hour of our faith, we have heard, wafting obscurely through the din of Christian conversation, the narratives of near-death. They are metaphors, perhaps, mere allegories, or not--but still the narratives persist, in part because the theme of resurrection is intrinsically a Christian one. It is part of us all. We all play some distinctive role, however infinitesimal, in telling it anew. It is a perennial, if not an eternal, story. In the words of one medieval NDE researcher, "What we describe is neither new nor incredible."[1]

Among contemporary chroniclers of the near-death experience, one of the most significant voices is that of Carol Zaleski. Her books, *Otherworld Journeys*: *Accounts of Near-Death Experience in Medieval and Modern Times*, *The Life of the World to Come*: *Near-Death Experience and Christian Hope*, and *The Book of Heaven*, as well as many articles, lend particular attention to the implication of near-death narratives for contemporary Catholics.

Zaleski does this openly and via implication, directing readers to consider Church tradition, scripture, and the impact of collective faith imagination. Her synthesis of these suggests a spiritual perspective that is faithful without being stale and that may be employed in daily life and in our spiritual retreat. Indeed, Zaleski's writing is sufficiently poetic to effect within the reader the experience of feeling, understanding, *and* employing this perspective, in a single seamless act.

Early Christian Precedents

Zaleski cites as the earliest reference to what might have been a Christian NDE, that of the apostle Paul in 2 Cor. 12:1-4, wherein the apostle claims to have known "a man in Christ," traditionally assumed to be himself, who was caught up to the third heaven and who "heard things that cannot be told, which man may not utter." Zaleski notes that evidence of deviation from the standard format of a "vision" is Paul's ambiguity concerning the exact dynamics of his spiritual experience--whether he had truly died ("whether in the body or out of the body I do not know") or not.

Zaleski gives significant attention to some extra-scriptural accounts of Christian NDE and NDE-related experience, such as the "Vision of St. Paul," which Zaleski deems to be the seminal example of this genre. This document first surfaced in the third century and purports to be a scrupulous disclosure of Paul's curious experience. However, Zaleski points out that belief in Pauline authorship was not unanimous among the early Christian fathers. She notes "St. Augustine's refusal to believe that the apostle would have disclosed the very secrets that he himself had deemed 'unlawful to utter.'"[2]

What "Paul" does describe are elements that later would become the staples of medieval Christian near-death narratives. For instance, he witnesses the exit of three souls from their bodies and then proceeds to follow their transitions. In one, the specter of a righteous man departs his body and is met by angels, who fend off an attack by devils and who usher him to heaven.

In another case, a wicked man is forcibly and painfully extracted from his body by "angels without mercy," who claim him as a comrade and escort him into hell. In a third, the narrator observes a man whose own guardian angel suddenly "turns state's evidence" by supplying documented evidence of the man's guilt and by calling forth as witnesses the souls of individuals that he had wronged.[3]

Medieval Accounts

Zaleski also draws upon the *Dialogues* of Gregory the Great, the sixth-century pope, spiritual writer, and Christian near-death researcher. In *Otherworld Journeys*, she recounts some memorable near-death anecdotes contained within the *Dialogues*. In one, Gregory reveals the testimony of an interviewee named Stephen. According to Gregory, Stephen was a businessman who had always doubted the existence of a hell, until he died while on a trip to Constantinople.

Gregory tells us that Stephen reports arriving at the judgment seat, but staying only briefly. Echoing a theme that has continued in near-death literature from medieval times until today, Stephen hears these words: "I ordered Stephen the blacksmith to be brought here, not this man." But as Zaleski points out, Gregory insists that such apparent mix-ups are intentional, meant to be a form of warning.[4]

Another anecdote involves a hermit who awakens from the dead and then proclaims that he has been to hell, where he had seen some prominent officials suffering the torments of the damned. According to Gregory, the hermit even tells of being dragged into the flames himself, escaping only by angelic hand. He is returned to physical existence with the sobering advice: "Leave, and consider carefully how you will live from now on."[5]

In examining the literature of Christian near-death experience, Zaleski recognizes that in medieval narratives the theme of punishment predominates. Consequently, so too do the descriptions of a population and of landscapes synonymous with hell. However, it should be noted that Zaleski's work, though reflective of this penitential focus, is studded with the imagery of heaven.

For example, in this passage from the *Dialogues*, quoted by Zaleski, Gregory recounts the testimony of a soldier who had died in Rome and who later was revived:

> He said that there was a bridge, under which ran a
> black, gloomy river which breathed forth an intolerably
> foul-smelling vapor. But across the bridge there were

delightful meadows carpeted with green grass and sweet-smelling flowers. The meadows seemed to be meeting places for people clothed in white. Such a pleasant odor filled the air that the sweet smell by itself was enough to satisfy [the hunger of] the inhabitants who were strolling there.[6]

Zaleski also gives significant attention to another near-death Church tradition in her article "St. Patrick's Purgatory: Pilgrimage Motifs in a Medieval Otherworld Vision." Located in Lough Derg, in the modern-day Irish county of Donegal, this popular pilgrimage site was traditionally believed to have been founded in the fifth century A.D., although it remained a much-frequented destination for pilgrims throughout the Middle Ages.

In her article, Zaleski recounts that the "purgatory" was believed to be a physical opening in the surface of the earth that led down to, among other things, the contiguous realms of hell and purgatory proper. A pilgrim would be locked--alone--inside the cave-like cell, and if the pilgrim could survive this terrible experience, it was assumed that he or she was to be spared the more extended trip to purgatory after death.[7]

Perhaps the best known of the purgatory's narratives is that of the knight Owen. In this extract, Zaleski recounts the conclusion of his journey:

> His ordeals behind him, Owen walks up to a jeweled gate, which opens in welcome, leading him to a land of light more dazzling than the sun, where he meets a procession of clergy carrying crosses, banners, candles, and golden palm branches, and singing an unearthly harmony. Two archbishops take Owen on a tour of the delightful meadows adorned with flowers, fruit, grass, and trees, "on whose fragrance he felt he could subsist forever."[8]

Zaleski gives particular attention to the imagery contained within the narrative of Drythelm, the seminal example of a genre that Zaleski calls the "Drythelm Line," which she argues is distinguished by the pattern of death, revival, and conversion. According to Bede the Venerable in his *Ecclesiastical History of the English People*, Drythelm was a righteous family man in eighth-century Northumbrian England, who died by illness. Bede writes that on the next day after he had died, Drythelm suddenly revives, sitting up abruptly on his deathbed, and horrifying those around him.[9] In *Otherworld Journeys*, Zaleski renders some descriptions of Drythelm's hellish tour--but as Zaleski's choice of extracts underscores, the imagery in Drythelm is not wholly negative.

For example, in the final stages of his tour, Drythelm is joined by an ethereal guide, who leads him further on. Soon Drythelm and his guide approach a massive wall, which, in an instant, they ascend. Atop the wall they stand amid a luminous, flower-strewn meadow, where Drythelm encounters "many companies of happy people." He believes himself to be in heaven, but soon discovers that it is only an "antechamber" of heaven "for the not quite perfect." Nearing heaven proper, Drythelm is rapt by the combined allure of ethereal singing, heavenly light, and an irresistibly sweet fragrance. Despite his urge to stay, he is sent back to his body, with the word that righteous living will make possible his ultimate return to paradise.[10]

Pastoral visions of heaven, such as those described by Drythelm, are not at all uncommon in the body of Zaleski's work. Additionally, in examining Zaleski's work we easily discover that such imagery is not found solely in medieval stories of near-death. Indeed, Zaleski notes some striking similarities between medieval and contemporary variations. In relating a contemporary NDE account of such illumined imagery, Zaleski writes that one woman "stepped into a realm of more 'subtle' illumination, a flowery meadow saturated with colors she had never seen before."[11]

It soon becomes apparent that the element of color is intrinsic to Zaleski's work, as in her choice to quote contemporary writer Karlis Osis: "They [modern experiencers] see nonearthly environments characterized by light, beauty, and intense color."[12] Through exquisite use of language, Zaleski renders this illumined imagery, transcending history and distance:

Nearly every witness to this heavenly region speaks of colors in this way; one man describes them as the colors of Utopia, the perfect originals of which earthly hues are only a copy. Along with verdant lawns, pure blue sky and lakes, and a mixed pallet of flowers and rainbows, the otherworld is ornamented with the colors of precious metals and jewels mined from the empyrean.[13]

Zaleski is aware that such a focus on imagination and perception might imply a dream-like model of the world to come. But she reminds us that the typical returnee from an NDE describes a world that is "startlingly lucid," perhaps even more real than physical existence. In *The Life of the World to Come: Near-Death Experience and Christian Hope*, she writes:

It is as if they [NDE experiencers] were given, within a dream, an intimation of what it would be like to be fully awake. And this intimation accords with a fundamental feature of Christian eschatological hope. What Christians hope for, finally, is a collective awakening, an entry into a real world, compared to which our present world is almost fallen into non-being.[14]

Conclusion

The thought and imagery conveyed within this little book outline potentially new dimensions for the function of imagination in contemporary Catholic life, which I hope have been effectively displayed for the retreatant. Far from being unfamiliar, the contours of this vision are distinct, synthesizing the Johannine theme of God as holy light, the venerable traditions of the Church, and the affirmation of the Christian free will as revealed within the spiritual and theological imagination. This all appears to be fresh grist for Catholic discussion. Such discussion may yield greater realization of the Gospel in renewal. Evidence of such a realization might be manifested in a freshly renewed outlook on external possibilities.

In *Otherworld Journeys*, Zaleski writes that "a sudden sense of inward illumination can spill over into the landscape, saturating it with beauty, light, newness, vitality, and harmony." To illustrate this point, she cites an interviewee quoted by the writer William James in his study of conversion:

> It was like entering another world, a new state of existence. Natural objects were glorified, my spiritual vision was so clarified that I saw beauty in every material object in the universe, the woods were vocal with heavenly music; my soul exulted in the love of God, and I wanted everybody to share in my joy.[15]

Such imagery befits the shimmering landscapes of the Catholic spiritual imagination. It epitomizes the essence of the Christian return-from-death experience and of Christian spirituality overall, that of renewed community and nature. It is the perennial message of Easter, infusing our song, our liturgy, and our sense of continuity. The aim of this retreat companion is to help facilitate this inward sense of spiritual renewal in the Catholic retreatant. I hope that this effect has been experienced, and that, in this changing season of the Church, it will spill over into the landscape of the Catholic desiring renewal.

Notes

1. Zaleski, Carol. *Otherworld Journeys: Accounts of Near-Death Experience in Medieval and Modern Times.* (Oxford: Oxford University Press, 1987), p. 85. Hereafter referred to as *Otherworld.*
2. Ibid., p. 26.
3. Ibid., p. 27.
4. Ibid., p. 29.
5. Ibid., p. 29.
6. Ibid., p. 29.
7. "St. Patrick's Purgatory: Pilgrimage Motifs in a Medieval Otherworld Vision." *Journal of the History of Ideas.* Vol. XLVI. No. 4. (1985), pp. 467, 469-470.
8. Ibid., p. 476.
9. *Otherworld*, p. 31.
10. Ibid., p. 32.
11. Ibid., p. 134.
12. Ibid., p. 113.
13. Ibid., p. 134.
14. *The Life of the World to Come: Christian Near-Death Experience and Christian Hope.* (Oxford: Oxford University Press, 1996), p. 67.
15. *Otherworld*, p. 200.

Printed in the United States
39271LVS00002B/4-30

9 781413 782868